FIND MY BABY!

The Inside Story of
Valiree Jackson

John W. Stone

The Exposure Publishing
A Division of The Grand Opening Shopper Company

The Exposure Publishing

A Division of The Grand Opening Shopper Company
6740 W. Deer Valley Road, Ste. D-107 #204
Glendale, AZ 85310-5953

ISBN 0-929526-15-5

Cover design © 2000 by Shirley D. Stone

First paperback printing May 2000

Printed in the United States of America

www.phoenixpublishinggroup.com

It were better for him that a millstone were hanged about his neck, and he cast into the sea, than that he should offend one of these little ones.
-Luke 17:2

TABLE OF CONTENTS

TABLE OF CONTENTS (CONT.)

Acknowledgements

I would like to give thanks to the following individuals and businesses. Their work, comfort, support, and prayers will always be remembered.

Thanks to: Sheriff Sterk, Captain Simmons, Sergeant Goodwin, Lieutenant Silver, Sheriff's Spokesperson Dave Reagan, and the individuals with Search and Rescue; the members of Calvary Baptist Church and their Pastor, Reverend C.W. Andrews, Redeemer Lutheran Church and Elder Sandy Anderson, and the members of Valley Fourth Memorial Church; the entire staffs at the Spokane Valley Quality Inn Suites, the Fairfield Inn, and the Pheasant Hill Best Western; Gerald Nicodemus, Robin Kieffer and the staff of the Two Rivers Casino and Resort; Todd Samuels, Jeff Wells and the staff of Spokane Indian Bingo and Casino; Coeur D'Alene Tribal Bingo and Casino; Brad Martin and the employees at Martin's Auto Service; all the employees at Sturm Heating and Air Conditioning, and the entire personnel at Longhorn Barbecue.

I appreciate the Spokane media for their stupendous coverage; Trova Hutchins, Debra Armstrong, and Ava Becks, reporters from KXLY TV, the ABC affiliate; Jeff Humphrey and Scott Charelston reporters from KREM, the CBS affiliate; Gary Darigold and Peter Alexander reporters from KHQ

TV, the NBC affiliate; FOX 28 News and reporter Kirsten Joyce, and the staff of the Spokesman Review, the Spokane Newspaper, KXLY radio hosts Mike Fitzsimmons, Mark Fuhrman, and Paul Seebeck.

In addition, I would like to thank the following personnel of the grocery stores in the states of Washington and Idaho: Safeway, Rosauers, Tidyman's, and Yokes; also Mike Proulx, Sonny Day and the other personnel with Bashas' in Arizona; retail stores Kmart and Wal-Mart, as well as the many stores and businesses who allowed us to post Valiree's and Roseann's picture; the administrators of the schools, their teachers and students who prayed for Valiree's safe recovery.

Special thanks to Steve and Jodel Frank, Molly, Bob, Scott, Kevin, and Shelly Egeland. Also, a special thanks to Marilyn Dugger, a friend of the family who has continued to stay in touch with the Spokane police regarding Roseann.

Thanks to my brother James, his wife Janice and my brother Rufus for their love and support. Thanks to my dad for his strength and to my nieces and nephews. Thanks to Roseann's children Joktan, Cynarra, and Angelica. Thanks to my sisters Kathy and Mary and to my aunt and uncle, Roberta and Mike Quiggle.

I appreciate the love and support from my five sons, Rodney, Sabron, Jonathan, Damian, and Timothy and for their ongoing prayers.

Last, but not least, an affectionate thanks to my wife Shirley, for her love, support, inspiration, and help in writing this book.

FOREWORD

I knew in 1992 that my sister Roseann was having problems in her relationship with Brad Jackson. Roseann's life with Brad was a living hell. There was physical and emotional abuse. After the birth of their daughter Valiree, their problems escalated.

Our mother became very suspicious after not hearing from Roseann after a week had gone by. Roseann always checked in with her, either by telephone or in person. She knew all about Roseann's troublesome relationship with Brad and knew Roseann feared for Valiree's safety. After a week had passed and she still had no word from Roseann, she became worried.

She told me that Valiree's second birthday would be in a few days and if she was all right, she knew that she would not miss her baby's birthday. But she did.

The police had few leads. They questioned Brad, but he refused to take the lie-detector test. Months before Roseann mysteriously disappeared, she was called to the morgue to identify a girlfriend who had been murdered. Roseann was very upset about this and was scared for her own life. For some reason, she wouldn't say why.

When mother called me to come and help find Roseann, I immediately got on the plane to Spokane. My brother James joined me to help in the search. We went around to churches and businesses to post flyers. For over a week we tried and tried to find our sister. We searched and searched, but no Roseann.

It was out of character for her to not be in touch with someone. Her uncashed check and all her belongings were left behind.

After a short while, my sister's case was placed with other cases of women whose deaths were attributed to a serial killer. We became discouraged and returned home, hoping that Roseann would show-up soon.

After I returned home to Phoenix, I kept praying that I would hear from her. It seemed that everywhere I looked, someone would remind me of her. A smile, the way they wore their hair, any little thing would cause the yearning to see my sister again.

As time went on, I started having dreams of her— dreams and visions that I didn't comprehend. During this last year they became more frequent and at times, eerie. Since the dreams had become a frequent occurrence, I didn't pay much attention to them; I couldn't decipher their meaning.

Now looking back at that time, all those feelings of frustration and guilt have overwhelmed me. Why didn't I stay longer in Spokane to look for Roseann? Why didn't I pay more attention to the dreams? Were the dreams some kind of message from her, or was it just my overwhelming desire to see her again?

It was 7 years ago, the last time Valiree's mother was seen.

Sadly, I believe that what happened to my niece also happened to my sister.

This book is a personal account of what I went through. It is about the confusion, turmoil, and contradictions which I had to face not once, but twice.

What is written in this book represents my own opinions and memories during the time of October 18th thru December 17, 1999. I was absent from some of the events that I describe. However, I was given accounts from people who were there and the news media. Other descriptions were created from my own interpretation of what could have happen.

I was determined to find out what happened to my niece. I was determined to find a resolution for my sister. For the unsolved mysteries that remain, I am still determined to find the answers.

"I Can't Find Valiree!"

"By God, by God, I can't find Valiree!"

Brad, Valiree Jackson's father, ran across the street from his home on Blossey Avenue to a neighbor's house in the Spokane Valley.

He was banging on her door and yelling, "By God, by God, I can't find Valiree!"

That was 8:40, Monday morning, October 18, 1999.

"What are you talking about?"

The neighbor saw Brad was shaking and crying.

"Calm down and tell me what happened."

"I can't find Valiree!"

He explained that he was doing a load of laundry inside, and knew Valiree was playing outside in the backyard with the dog.

"But when I went to walk her to school, I couldn't find her!"

"Did you hear anything?" she asked.

"Yeah, I heard the garage door open. I just thought she was going to the front yard to wait for me. She goes that way all the time— through the garage."

1

"Did you look in the house again?"

"She wasn't in the front yard. I called her name but she didn't come. I looked in the back yard, the garage, and the house— calling her name, but I didn't get an answer. Then, when I found her back-pack on the front steps, I didn't know what to do!"

Brad was still shaking and crying.

"Valiree's gone. All I found was her back pack on the front steps."

The female neighbor contacted some other nearby neighbors and together they thoroughly searched the area for several minutes.

No Valiree.

Around 8:45, Brad called 911.

The Spokane Sheriff's Department assigned six detectives with three trained dogs on the case immediately. About thirty volunteers rushed to the side to help find 9-year old Valiree. Brad stayed home.

❀ ❀ ❀

The Grieving Father

A sheriff's deputy stood guard outside the house while the news media waited for Brad to give them a picture of Valiree.

Shelly, a neighbor of the Jacksons was a crossing guard and teacher's assistant at Valiree's school. She lived two and a half blocks from the Jacksons. When she arrived home that morning she received a phone call from her mother-in-law, Molly Egeland.

"Valiree is missing!"

Stunned and worried, Molly and Shelly hastily finished their phone conversation. Molly set out to help in the search. Shelly went over to console the grieving father.

Shelly arrived at the Jackson's home about 9:10 and spent the following six hours with Brad and his mother, Karen.

Karen and Wilbur, Brad's father, left that morning around 4:30. Wilbur worked in Portland, Oregon. Karen dropped Wilbur off at the airport and went to her job at Pathology Associates in town.

Karen returned home from work that morning after hearing the devastating news that her granddaughter was missing. She was visibly upset and wanted Valiree home safe.

Karen said that she had kissed Valiree goodbye when leaving that morning around 4:30.

She and Valiree had plans that afternoon to bake cookies.

While the community was searching for Valiree, a detective questioned Brad about what happened that morning. After he had finished questioning Brad he walked out the front door. Brad closed the door behind him, showing that he was furious. He raised his voice sharply, "I am !#%* upset that that !#%* detective is making me out as a !#%* suspect." He didn't care for the police or the media. He wasn't exactly doing his best to cooperate.

There was an instance when Karen ran into the kitchen crying hysterically. She leaned against the counter sobbing uncontrollably, then slowly slid to the floor in a heap. Brad, seeing her that way, ran over, grabbed her abruptly, and pulled her up speaking to her harshly. He then turned and smiled at Shelly and said, "Even if the police suspect me, I'm sticking to my story." He even sang the words "That's my story and I'm sticking to it."

Brad then led Shelly to the doorway of Valiree's room. He showed her Valiree's pillow with bloodstains. The blood had soaked through the pillowcase into the pillow as well.

Brad told Shelly that Valiree was having, "Dreams of monsters coming after her." He emphasized that the monster coming after her was her mother and that the dreams caused Valiree's bloody noses.

Shelly was bewildered as to why Brad was showing her those things.

❀ ❀ ❀

Where's Valiree?

The deputies searched the Jackson home twice.

The deputies checked with the school officials at Valiree's school, McDonald Elementary. The school was several blocks away. Brad walked her to school often.

When Jan, Valiree's principal was told the news about Valiree, she became visibly upset. Jan saw Valiree as part of her family, so to speak. She and her staff were devastated. They told the detective that Valiree was a pleasure to be around.

She was "a bright, happy, well-adjusted little girl."
She had no history of running away, no problems at school, and no known serious conflicts with her family. Detectives talked to friends and classmates, but no one had a clue where Valiree was.

"She's a sweet, friendly little girl."

Around noon, a larger search began. It covered a 24-square-block area near Pines Road. The searchers went house to house, block by block.

Although Brad seemed shaken, individuals at the scene said that he didn't give the media a picture of Valiree for a number of hours. When the media did get the picture, they broadcast it on the news while copies were passed out.

Valiree's neighbors and others in the community searched the area along with personnel from the Sheriff's department and Search and Rescue.

Where was Valiree? Where was that happy, brown-eyed, curly red-haired little girl that was sometimes playfully called Annie? Where was that 4-foot-8, 73- pound bundle of joy? Had anyone seen the precious little girl with blue jeans, a white turtleneck with cute little teddy bears, and a bright pink jacket with pretty blue hearts?

Her father seemed devastated.

The Dreams

Later that evening I received the news about Valiree.

R-r-ring. R-r-ring.

I answered to the voice of my sister, Kathy who lived in Spokane.

"Winnie," she said, using my childhood nickname, growing up, "Valiree's been abducted from her home! Her picture is all over the news!"

"This can't be! No, no, this can't be!" I told her. "Are you sure it's Valiree? Kathy, are you sure?"

Kathy was crying, "Yes, Winnie I'm sure. What should we do? Winnie, please tell me what to do?"

I was shocked.

Kathy asked, "Do you think Roseann has her? Winnie, do you think our sister is still alive?" We both wanted that so much.

"Kathy, keep me informed of everything that's happening there and I'll get in touch with James," I said, referring to our older brother.

After I got off the phone with Kathy, I called James at his home in Laguna Niguel, California.

"James, Valiree has been abducted!" Alarmed, he asked me if I had confirmed the abduction with the police. I told him it was confirmed, her picture was on the news.

We all clung to the hope that Roseann was alive. We wanted our sister to be alive so bad.

Seven years ago, around this time, Roseann disappeared without a trace. Now it was happening all over again. We have had no clues— nothing. Her disappearance was a total mystery.

We asked each other, "How could this be possible?" We were fearful and doubtful, we didn't want to believe that anyone other than Roseann had Valiree. The thought of her having Valiree was a lot more comforting than anything else, but we were puzzled at the same time. We didn't want to believe that something like this could happen in our family, certainly not twice.

That night I tossed and turned, living a nightmare. In my mind I kept seeing my sister alive, playing with her baby. I hoped and prayed that Roseann was alive. I prayed that Valiree was all right too and that she would return home soon.

The perplexing dreams I had been having were now beginning to have meaning, but I didn't want to believe that they meant that Roseann wasn't alive.

In one dream, Roseann was beckoning me, she was saying, "find my baby, find my baby." I dismissed it because I knew that Roseann's three older children were okay and that Brad had Valiree. However, after hearing about Valiree's abduction, I became frightened. I wanted to believe that Roseann had Valiree, but were my dreams telling me something else?

I awakened many nights with haunting dreams of Roseann. I always told my wife about them and we had many conversations trying to determine their meaning. My wife believes that dreams are images from our subconscious mind and that they sometimes have meaning, but the meaning of those particular dreams eluded us. They were strange to me.

I hadn't heard or seen Roseann for seven years, so I just concluded that the dreams had come from a yearning that I had to see her again. We thought that if Roseann was alive, then why would she be giving me those instructions? Were the dreams really instructions?

I wanted to believe that she had escaped death, that she wasn't murdered. On the other hand, I couldn't imagine her just leaving her family, and her children.

Were they real— you know the dreams? Were they telling me something about the future?

Certainly I couldn't physically see these dreams, so why would I think they were real? I would soon find out that my dreams were very much real. Just as King Nebuchadnezzar found out how real his dreams were from the dream interpreter Daniel, a biblical character.

Roseann and Brad

Roseann and Brad both grew up in and around Spokane. For the most part our family lived on the north side of town.

There was a total of eight in our immediate family. Our dad, Reverend Rufus Stone, was a devout churchgoer. He is a Black American. Our mother, Helen Louise Pappas Stone, was Greek, Irish, Danish, and German. There were three boys including me and three girls including Roseann. Roseann and I were the closest in age. She was 11 months younger than I and the oldest girl.

Roseann didn't get into judging people by their color. She dated based on how she felt about the guy and how the guy treated her. She knew that her skin color was brown, but she believed that the inner person was colorless. We all dated different races— we were boomers. We didn't let color or traditions stand in our way; anyway, how would that look? We were and are proud of our different heritage.

Roseann graduated from Rogers High School in 1975. She was liked by almost everyone who knew her. She and I were in the same grade, since my mom had held me back after struggling in first grade.

In school, Roseann was the quiet one while I was the show-off. As we got older, like most kids, we talked to each other about what we wanted to be when we grew up.

When Roseann was a little girl, she often talked about being a nurse. As we got older she decided that she wanted to be a court reporter. She would tell me, "Winnie I'm going to be a court reporter and I don't want to see you in court." We both laughed.

After Roseann graduated from high school she met Jim who was several years older than her. Together they decided to attend the University of New Mexico in Albuquerque. Shortly after starting college, Roseann became pregnant with Joktan, her first-born. She decided to leave school hoping someday to return and finish her college education. For now she was to become a mother.

Roseann and Jim split-up and she returned to Spokane to raise her son. Upon her return, she and I rented an apartment together. We had many discussions about the future. She didn't want her child raised without a father.

Shortly after moving in together, Roseann met Don Pleasant. After dating Don for a while, they got married. She was so happy. I remember her telling me how she was going to be the best wife and mother.

Roseann had learned how to take care of a family at a very young age. As children, our mother was sick quite often and Roseann was counted on to help my dad take care of my mother and the rest of the family. Having her own family, she desired to be the perfect homemaker.

After she and Don were married, they lived in Kennewick, Washington. Don had a job that kept him out of town quite often. For a while they were a perfect family.

Roseann became pregnant with their first child together, and it appeared that their marriage was better than ever. But shortly after the birth of her second child Cynarra, problems arose in their marriage that caused Roseann to regret not finishing college.

Roseann loved Don but the marriage just didn't work. Their marriage ended but they remained friends. Being a mother without a husband was not something Roseann wanted. She wanted a relationship but she wasn't about to make a compromise that involved her children for anyone.

From 1985 to 1989, Roseann found herself in and out of relationships. One of those relationships was with Mike, a man she met while attending church. For a while it appeared that they were headed to the altar. Roseann got pregnant and she and Mike had a beautiful baby girl whom they named Angelica. Shortly after Angelica's birth, Mike and Roseann permanately separated. Roseann had three children to provide for and she did just that. Her children were so well behaved and loved. They knew that their mom loved them.

In mid 1989, Roseann met Brad Jackson. She was overjoyed. She told me that he was her prince charming. She saw Brad as an adventurer and someone exciting to be with.

Brad, one of Wilbur and Karen Jackson's three children, graduated from Riverside High School in Chattaroy, Washington. Chattaroy is about 14 miles north of Spokane. Out of the graduating class of about 100, Brad was said to have been the most dedicated.

Brad's classmates described him as a quiet and aloof person. After high school Brad held several different jobs, including working in the maintenance department at the Spokane airport. He also was a truck driver for Haskins Steel Company.

Prior to meeting Roseann, Brad had been engaged to a woman named Becky. For some reason their engagement was called off and Brad tried to fill the void with different women.

Brad met Roseann when he was 22 years old. She was 31. A friend of Brad's remembers their first week together.

"Brad and Roseann were flying down the street on his motorcycle and they pulled up in my yard. They looked so happy. Brad introduced us and we immediately bonded. Roseann was very loving.

Several months after they met, Roseann became pregnant. I lived only a block or so away from them. I would walk over to their house to visit Roseann, and Brad, answering the door, told me, "not now." I found it strange that Roseann stayed in the house so much when she became pregnant. Roseann's other children seemed to always be cared for, so I minded my own business. I really thought Brad and Roseann loved each other."

During Roseann's pregnancy, Brad began to beat her. Roseann didn't know why Brad would get so enraged. She thought maybe it was because he thought the baby would have dark skin. He called her nigger on occasions and told her that he did not want a nigger child. It was during this time that Brad told her about his father.

He said that his father was prejudice and that he wouldn't accept a dark-skinned child. Roseann told me that Brad was very fearful of his dad. She didn't know what Brad would do if the baby was dark. She thought that if the baby had fair skin like Brad's, then they would be happy together.

Boy, was she wrong! Roseann got a short reprieve from Brad's abuse during the last months of her pregnancy. She thought it was because he had decided to accept the baby regardless of its color.

On October 6, 1990, Roseann gave birth to Valiree Brianne Jackson. She was elated that the baby was healthy. She would love and take care of the child regardless of what Brad felt. However, the joy of the birth of their daughter would be short-lived.

The arguments and beatings started up again. Roseann didn't know what to do. She felt so trapped, all she wanted was for Brad to accept her and her children. But that never happened. So she turned to drugs for relief.

She was very familiar with prescription drugs. As a child there were many times when she had to give our mother her medication. She used to tell me how mom needed her pills to make the hurt go away. Since Brad was not giving her what she needed, she began to seek affection elsewhere.

By the time Valiree was 3 months old, Brad and Roseann were no longer living together. Brad started his campaign to get custody of Valiree. Roseann was beside herself. She knew in her heart that Brad didn't really love Valiree. Since he couldn't beat up on her anymore, she thought he was trying to hurt her by getting custody of Valiree.

Brad had a plan to get custody of Valiree. He decided to use Roseann's dependence on drugs against her. It didn't seem to matter that he was an avid drug user himself. Roseann and her attorney fought the system to keep custody, but to no avail.

Roseann felt terrible when the court gave Brad temporary custody of Valiree. She still had her other children and was given a chance to clean up her habit and regain custody of Valiree.

Brad would have none of this. Valiree's skin was white and Brad wouldn't have her raised around Roseann's darker-complexioned children. He believed that she would fit right in with his family. She was only one quarter black and by looking at her, Brad believed no one could tell.

For most of 1991 and 1992, Roseann and Brad fought back and forth. They didn't have to live together to fight. Brad wanted this for Valiree and Roseann wanted that. Roseann wanted Brad's family to accept that she was Valiree's mother. Brad didn't want that. She told me that it was like Brad wanted Valiree to forget her altogether.

14

The court set up visitations for Roseann to be with Valiree. Brad supervised the visits. She said that Brad would just snatch Valiree away from her for no reason whatsoever and then abruptly leave. The visits were always short and nasty. She hated his control.

During our family reunion in the summer of 1992, Roseann tearfully confided to me that she was afraid that Brad was trying to take Valiree out of her life completely. She was going back to court to get her baby back, whatever the cost.

I told Roseann that she needed to get as far away from Brad as she could. He was nothing but trouble for her and that she was smart, attractive, and capable of putting her life back together without any man. I told her that she could come to Phoenix and work for our company and earn a very good salary.

In mid September of 1992, Roseann called me to tell me that she was going to take me up on my offer. My wife and I had invited Roseann to bring her children to live and work with us in Phoenix. We wanted to help her and her children. We owned an advertising company and had a job waiting for her.

Roseann said, she told Brad that she was going to get Valiree back. She also let Brad know that she was planning to attend Valiree's second birthday on October 6. She was very adamant about it. That was a major problem. The party was to be at Brad's parent's home and Roseann was not invited.

On September 29, 1992, Roseann had a supervised visit with Valiree at Mission Park in Spokane. As far as we know, Brad was the last person to see her. That was the last time anyone saw Roseann—that we know of.

Brad told police detective Don Giese that he had given Roseann a ride after their visit. Brad claimed he dropped my sister off at the corner of Nora and Ash, on the West Side of Spokane. We had no idea what happened to Roseann and neither, said Brad, did he.

Don Giese being suspicious of Brad, asked him to take a lie-detector test, but he refused. Our mother was beside herself. She wanted the police to search his car and his different residences. At first she would call Giese daily. She told me that the police began to hang-up on her because of her persistence. In fact, there were many times that she would call the police and they would put her on hold and never come back to the telephone. Their neglect in my sister's disappearance was too much for my mother to take. All she wanted was her daughter back and the right to see Valiree.

Here I was on October 18, 1999, living my sister's mysterious disappearance all over again. However, this time it's her daughter Valiree, who's mysteriously disappeared.

❀ ❀ ❀

Where's Uncle John?

On Tuesday, October 19th, I called the Spokane's Sheriff Department for an update. They told me, no news on Valiree yet. Dave Reagan, the Sheriff Spokesperson kept everyone updated.

I was told that it was as though Valiree had disappeared into thin air.

While interviewing potential witnesses, detectives discovered an attempted abduction of a 13-year-old Spokane Valley girl around noon on Saturday.

Apparently, a man offered the girl cigarettes, marijuana, and money to get into his flatbed truck. That happened on South Sullivan Road, a site less than two miles from Valiree's neighborhood. Not much else turned up.

Posters asking if anyone had seen Valiree were now being distributed in outlying communities, including Newport and the Idaho towns of Priest River and Sandpoint. Grocery Stores, along with Wal-Mart and Kmart, were the best locations to hang Valiree's posters. The people who work in the stores were a great help.

I wanted so badly to leave my home and go to Spokane immediately, but I couldn't. I had commitments and had to put everything in order before leaving.

I contacted Valiree's half- sister Cynarra. Cynarra is Roseann and Don Pleasant's oldest daughter. I told her to contact printing businesses in Spokane to see if they would help us get posters of Valiree printed.

Cynarra was very helpful. She wanted so desperately to find her sister. For seven years they had been separated.

Cynarra and my sisters Kathy and Mary, along with her daughters Tasha and Kascedra, set out to spread the news about Valiree's abduction. My nephews, Kathy's sons, Terral and Calvin-pitched in. They went to the malls and the stores and vocalized the need for help and posted flyers.

The Spokane media was always there for us, they were more than helpful. They were encouraging and supportive beyond the call of duty. They seemed to take our ordeal personally.

I got a call from the Spokane newspaper, "The Spokesman Review."

"Did you know that your sister is alive?"

The caller said that records showed that Roseann lived in an apartment in the 1300 block of North Madelia as a resident from November 1996 to June 1998.

Was I shocked! *Roseann's alive? She's the one who has Valiree!* The thought immediately popped in my mind.

When the voice at the other end told me the news, I had so much hope. This thing was coming together. Valiree was finally with her mother again. I would get to see my sister again.

For seven long years I beat myself up for not being there when Roseann needed me most. Now I would get another chance to be her big brother.

I called my dad and told him the news. I called my brother and sisters and told them the news. We were all happy.

Now I just had to get to Spokane, but I was afraid. I guess I was afraid to believe. You know, believe that my sister had just walked away. Afraid, because I didn't know if I had said or caused something to happen to alienate my sister from me.

❋ ❋ ❋

More Leads + More Days = No Valiree

Although the newspaper gave us the news about Roseann, we were still very confused. Surely Roseann would be found now, we thought.

The detectives had four or five weak leads by Wednesday, October 20th. The main ones had to do with the flatbed truck driver and the woman that said she saw Roseann last year.

My family and I were very interested in the woman who said she saw my sister. We had read about this witness and the reporter had called me with this news.

With that news we were hoping that Roseann and Valiree would be alive. We wanted to believe that Roseann was the one who abducted Valiree and that we would be hearing from them soon.

As more time went by, we became worried that this wasn't the case at all.

The Sheriff's Department came out and said that they had no reason to believe that Roseann was a player in Valiree's abduction.

Don Giese, the homicide detective assigned to Roseann's case in 1992, had turned up no leads since that time.

We just kept hoping and praying that Roseann was alive and that she had Valiree.

By Thursday, October 21st, the fourth day, more than 50 tips had been given the detectives about Valiree's possible whereabouts.

These leads directed them back to the Spokane Valley neighborhood where they began interviewing local sex offenders.

It was reported that the detectives found the names of 80 sex offenders who currently lived in a two-mile radius of Valiree's neighborhood.

Valiree's neighborhood has many wonderful people as well as beautiful homes. It is a neighborhood that seems to protect and love their children.

I later found out that sex offenders are categorized at levels one, two, and three. Valiree's neighborhood appeared to me to be rather safe.

On Friday, October 22nd, six detectives were pulled from a disaster-training exercise to join the six detectives already working on the case.

Still with 12 detectives and 50 leads, the Sheriff's Department ended up having no clues after five days.

Who took Valiree? Where was she? Why was she taken?

Some of the detectives and other department personnel began to take this case home with them. They were at their ends. They wanted Valiree found and they wanted her found alive. They had families too and felt the pain. Whatever suspicions they had about Valiree's abduction were not going to be made known, at least not yet.

Back to Square One

"If the little girl disappeared from the house, there may be evidence there."

That statement was printed in the 'The Spokesman Review', a local newspaper.

A search warrant was served on the Jackson's home, Valiree's home.

The detectives were looking for any clue. Maybe when Valiree was abducted, something was dropped and tracked into the Jackson home. Maybe this or maybe that. The detectives were relentless. "No matter what happened, this is a very critical scene."

Brad Jackson and his parents were not considered suspects. The detectives were just being thorough and I for one— appreciated that.

The Sheriff's Deputies arrived at Brad's house around 6:00 Saturday night on October 23rd. I was still in Arizona— still clinging to the hope that Roseann was still alive and had Valiree. I was still hoping for a call from Roseann.

Back in Spokane the deputies had closed off half the block while searching for clues. For more than five hours, technicians and detectives combed

Brad's residence. They searched the split-level house inside for trace evidence. They also searched thoroughly outside the home as well. They were looking for hair, clothing fibers, footprints, or any bloodstains that could be detected.

The investigators seized two vehicles parked outside. One was a four-wheel-drive Ford pick-up and the other a two-door Honda Accord.

Taped to the back windows of the Honda were two fliers announcing Valiree's disappearance.

"The Phoenix Rising"

Finally, I was off to Spokane. Although I was staying in touch with the sheriff's department and family members, I needed to be there.

I thought, that if I asked Roseann to come forward— that is, if she was alive— then she would. I needed to make my appeal to my sister. If not my sister, then whoever abducted my niece. If Roseann wasn't there, then I had to be the big brother and find Valiree, her baby.

I was afraid for Valiree. I was determined to find her. I had to find her! I thought that by finding Valiree, I would find out what happened to my sister.

I flew into Spokane on Southwest Airlines Tuesday, October 26th, at 8:10 in the evening.

My sister Kathy and her boyfriend Jeff met me at the airport. The Spokane television media was there to greet me as well.

Fox 28 News, KREM TV, KXLY, and KHQ, all had reporters at the airport. They asked me for a comment and about my plans.

I told them that I was there to assist the law-enforcement agencies and to comfort my family. I told them that I didn't believe that Brad would do anything to hurt his daughter.

Brad and I didn't care for each other, at all. I especially didn't care for the games he played with my sister. I wasn't coming out and accusing him of anything— yet.

I actually wanted to work with Brad in order to find Valiree. Even if it meant finding out about Roseann.

As my sister and Jeff drove me to their home, I began mapping out my strategy. Kathy and Jeff would play a part in my plan. I knew I could depend on my niece Cynarra and my ex-wife Jodel and her husband, Steve Frank. We were all good friends. My brother and his wife were encouraging. My dad and my wife gave me strength. Truth and Justice were on our side. God would see us through. With all the support, surely we would find Valiree.

❀ ❀ ❀

False Hope

"Yeah, I've seen her. She lived on the other side of the building, but moved out in early fall of 98."

The detectives were trying to find the north Spokane resident who said that Roseann lived in an apartment on North Madelia Street a year ago.

The detectives found that the apartment building was recently sold and they couldn't reach the former owners to check out last year's tenants. Apparently, the woman was mistaken.

Although this piece of news was devastating, I still held on to the hope that my sister would return with Valiree. My first order of business on Wednesday morning was to go to Brad's house and meet with him.

Jeff drove me downtown to rent a car from Rent-A-Wreck. Mitch the owner and his assistant James knew me from past business dealings. Their friendship and comfort were very much appreciated.

After getting the car, my niece, my sister, and I stopped for refreshments. Ava Beck, a news reporter from KXLY happened to be getting gas. She recognized me and asked me what were my plans. I told her that I was going out to talk with Brad in hope of forming a union to find my niece. She asked if she could tag along. I said certainly.

We arrived at Brad's house at about 9:00 that morning.

We knocked and knocked, and rang the doorbell, but no one answered.

I checked out the property and the surrounding area as well as I could. I tried to understand how Valiree's abduction could have happened.

I saw pictures of Valiree through the windows. I wondered why it took Brad so long to give the media a picture of her. What would I do, I wondered, if I was in Brad's shoes? Would I freeze?

I couldn't freeze. I couldn't panic. Not at the detriment of my child or any child.

As I stood by Brad's back fence, his dogs approached. I wished the dogs could tell me something. Surely they knew where Valiree was. I went back around to the front of the house.

I felt a presence in the house, so I knocked repeatedly but no one answered. I could feel a red-hot rage boiling inside of me. I scowled angrily and clenched my fists tightly at my sides. The pain in my hands was nothing compared to the pain I felt inside.

As I walked away from the front door of Brad's house, I looked back at the pictures hanging on the wall. Valiree captivated me with her beautiful smile. Her cropped red hair was a trait I found endearing. I refocused my thoughts saying,
"I'll find you Valiree, I'll find you."

Slowly I walked back to the car, contemplating my next move.

After leaving Brad's house I dropped my sister off at home and used her telephone. I called detective Giese to tell him that I was in town and would be down to see Roseann's file.

A news reporter had told me that my sister's file was closed and that I should be able to get a copy of it, or at least view it.

❋ ❋ ❋

Negligence

When I was 18, I worked for the police department as a crime check operator. I had seriously considered becoming a police officer. My supervisor at the time, and still considered a friend, was Sergeant Freeman.

As a crime check operator, I took incoming calls similar to those of the 911 operators. Sergeant Freeman was always trying to talk me into attending the Police Academy. He allowed me many opportunities to ride around with him and the officers to see what their work was all about.

When I walked into the Public Safety Building it seemed as though nothing had changed. I approached the front counter and asked the officers on duty for the Sheriff.

When I arrived in Spokane the day before, I mentioned to the news reporters that there was possibly some negligence involved in this case. This news broadcast went out on all the stations.

The officers had seen the news report and didn't seem to know how to take me. They didn't know if I was accusing them of negligence or someone else. They were apprehensive.

A sheriff's deputy came out and escorted me and my niece Cynarra, back to a conference room. We met with Captain Simmons, Sergeant Goodwin, and Lieutenant Silver. They stood on one side of the table with their arms folded and my niece and I stood on the other side.

We all sat down simultaneously. My niece was visibly upset. She wanted answers and she wanted them right then and there.

I reached out and gently held my niece's arm and began to tell the officers that I appreciated their hard work and diligence in Valiree's mysterious disappearance. I told them that I knew they got blamed for many things and that I was not there to blame them for Valiree's abduction. I knew they had families and children and that this ordeal had hit them hard as well.

With those comments, it was as though the tension had broken down between us. Captain Simmons was the first one to smile back at me, then Sergeant Goodwin and Lieutenant Silver smiled too.

I told them that the negligence that I was speaking about had to do with Brad's fiduciary duty as a parent, Valiree's parent. A duty a parent owes a child, a duty of care.

A duty to not freeze when your child needs you to act and act quickly.

A duty to get your child's picture out immediately.

In an abduction, time is everything.

I was talking about that negligence. I know we all react differently to emergencies. I wasn't blaming Brad for his inaction. We get scared and sometimes freeze. However, we are parents for a reason. Children are depending on mommy and daddy to be there for them, always.

My meeting with the officers went well. I was thankful that Valiree had those group of men and women working to find her.

They updated me and Cynarra on Valiree's case as much as they could. I knew that they had their own thoughts and suspicions that they couldn't share with us, so I didn't pressure them. They had a right to keep us in the dark about certain things; after all, they are the officers and that is part of their job. It doesn't mean that I always agree, I just respect it.

They told me that the city police were handling Roseann's case and that it was possible that she was a victim of the serial killer. *Yea, right*!

They knew that I believed that Brad had done something to my sister to cause her sudden and mysterious disappearance seven years ago.

I told them that it was possible that Brad had something to do with Valiree's abduction as well.

After our meeting we all stood up and exchanged business cards. We shook hands and wished each other well.

They told me that they knew that I would be out there conducting my own investigation and that any information I received could be forwarded to them.

I thanked them for their time and my niece and I left. From there, I drove to Kathy's house where I was staying. Thousands and thousands of fliers with Valiree's picture were passed out. Kathy, Cynarra, and I, along with many in the Spokane area, continued our quest to find Valiree.

❀ ❀ ❀

Let's Come Together

Brad was ready to take a lie-detector test.

"I'd like to get it done," he said.

He announced that on Monday evening, October 25.

Detectives offered to give Brad the test on Wednesday.

"Well, I'd have to think about it."

Think about what? This was his opportunity to eliminate himself as a potential suspect in his daughter's disappearance and he had to think about it?

"They haven't called me yet. They're supposed to call me."

Brad played this game with the police when my sister disappeared seven years ago. He never took the polygraph examination then, and I doubted whether he would take it now.

"I'd like them to shift the focus back to my daughter."

Scheduling the time to take the lie-detector test appeared to be the issue between the sheriff's department and Brad. The real issue however, was not when Brad would take the lie-detector test. It was if he would.

On Wednesday, October 27, the Spokane county deputies interviewed Brad. However, it was not clear at the time, whether he took the polygraph test or not.

After the meeting, the investigators withheld the results. When Brad was asked about the test, he had no comment. While he was silent, I was telling everyone in town that I wanted to work with him and the community to find Valiree.

After leaving the Sheriff's Department, we started out to the grocery stores, small businesses, office buildings, homes, and apartment buildings. We talked to people on the street, in restaurants, in clothing stores. We tacked the fliers on bulletin boards and telephone poles. We taped them on windows, doors, and we rang doorbells.

I had to get the word out about Valiree. I kept meeting people who had not heard about her disappearance. Maybe someone, somewhere would come forward and give us information. I knew that they were out there. I had to keep pounding, pounding, pounding away. I had an unrelenting desire to find Valiree.

I wanted Brad to open-up. Somehow I had to get him to talk to me. Although I had suspicions about Brad, I didn't want to publicly condemn him. I had to get Brad to believe in me.

On Thursday, October 28, I continued an all-day campaign to get more fliers out. I spent day and night talking to individuals and businesses, church leaders and organizations. I let them all know who Valiree Jackson was and solicited their help to find her.

Brad called Kathy's house to speak to Cynarra. This was the first time that anyone in our family had heard from Brad in years. We believed that he was hiding Valiree from us the past seven years.

"I have some pictures of your sister that I'd like to show you."

Brad told her that he would call her with a meeting place, but he never called back. We never saw the pictures.

Into the second week, there still was no breaking news concerning Valiree's case. Things were feeling hopeless.

I was afraid for Valiree. Every muscle in my face was aching. I began to feel frustrated just like I did seven years ago. I did not want to leave Spokane like this. I could hear the monotonous words, find my baby— find my baby, repeating in my head.

My suspicions about Brad began to grow. When I thought about him, a queasy uneasy feeling came over me. Something was not right, but I had to get his cooperation. I needed more media time. It was vital that I continue my pursuit to find Valiree.

❀ ❀ ❀

Leaving Spokane the First Time

In the meantime, Brad was gaining more sympathy and support from the community. He opened a bank account for which he received thousands of dollars from businesses and individuals for a reward to be paid for Valiree's return. Personally, I was too alarmed to feel sympathy for Brad just yet.

I figured that it might take weeks, possibly months to find Valiree. I began to drive by her house more frequently. I had driven through Valiree's neighborhood periodically since first arriving in Spokane. I thought that perhaps I could find some kind of clue, some hint about what happened to her.

Now it was time for me to return home, to Phoenix. My distrust for Brad had intensified. I wanted someone else to continue to watch him. Maybe someone would contact him about Valiree or maybe he would do something out of the ordinary. I didn't know what to expect from him or if he was stable.

I arranged with Kathy and Jeff, along with Steve and Jodel, to continue to drive through Brad's neighborhood and especially keep watch on the Jackson's house.

I had to get back to my family and business in Arizona. It was very challenging to juggle everything from such a distance. I had to get home and take care of matters that were pending. So, reluctantly, I made airline reservations to fly back to Phoenix on Friday.

I was not feeling very comfortable about leaving. Something wasn't right. I could sense it, but I had to leave for the time being.

I grabbed my sister's phone book to take with me. With it, I could still contact people by calling them from home. I needed to stay connected.

Before going to the airport, I stopped by the Spokane Police Department to look at Roseann's file. Don Giese, the homicide detective, who was working on Roseann's case after she disappeared in 1992, informed me that he would not be there, but I could talk to his superior, Captain Braun.

When I arrived at the station, I met with Captain Braun at the front counter. He found a room where he and I could sit down to discuss my sister's case privately.

The Captain preceded to tell me that I had been misinformed about my sister's file and that he was sorry for that. He said that Roseann's case was open and that her file had been placed with other unsolved cases of women believed to have been murdered by a serial killer. They were still trying to solve the serial killer cases and they were not having much success at the time.

This was not the first time that I had heard about this. It made me angry that my sister's case was classified as an unsolved murder without her body. To my knowledge, all the other women's bodies were found, but not Roseann's.

He said that something might turn up to link Roseann's and Valiree's cases together.

He implied that somehow Valiree's abduction was connected to the serial killer. I thought that was ludicrous.

Just because Roseann's case was unsolved didn't mean that Valiree's abduction had anything to do with the serial killer.

I told him that I suspected Brad in both cases. He said, I might be right.

I stepped back outside the police department and met the news reporters who gathered to ask me about my plans.

Feeling angry, I blurted out, Brad Jackson is a murderer! Trova Hutchins, the news reporter with KXLY, along with other reporters scrambled to turn off their microphones. Trova, with a concerned look said, "John you know we can't say that on the air, yet."

I proceeded to tell them that I was conducting my own investigation and that I was going home to put a report together regarding my findings.

I had no more answers than the sheriff's department. Perhaps I had a lot less than they had. I had only suspicions, but I thought that whoever was responsible for Valiree's abduction would think that I knew more than I was letting on.

I went to the airport that Friday afternoon and picked up my ticket at the Southwest Airline ticket counter for my flight to Phoenix. The agent told me that she recognized me from TV. She went on to tell me that at one time, Brad worked at the Spokane airport refueling planes. Many of the employees at the airport knew Valiree and they were all praying for her safe return.

I thanked her and headed for the gates. As I was standing in line to board the plane, a dad with his child walked up to me and put his arm around me. He told me that many people in the Spokane area were with me and to keep up the search for my niece and my sister. Several more people greeted me with a handshake and others with words of comfort. I was grateful for their support.

As I walked down the aisle to find my seat, a voice inside me whispered, *"Take care of what you have to and get back as soon as possible."*

The plane flew out of Spokane at 3:00 that afternoon. I felt very sad. I was trying to hold back my tears. The passenger next to me saw my tears and patted me on my shoulder.

"First time flying? Everything will be okay. You'll see."

He was trying to console me. I nodded without explanation as the tears rolled down my cheek. While looking out the window, I saw Spokane getting smaller and smaller— getting farther away.

Where can she be? Where is Valiree? Where is my sister? Where can they be?

✿ ✿ ✿

The Same Thing Can't Happen

I greeted my wife with a warm hug and kiss. I missed her and our life. I missed my boys.

"I have to get back. I have to return to Spokane as soon as possible."

It was good to be home again. I was happy that I could make the basketball game on Saturday for our youngest son. He was the same age as Valiree. I coached him with other eight, nine and ten-year-olds. I had done this for more than 10 years and was glad to have made another game.

As safe as we perceived our neighborhood to be, since Valiree's abduction, we would not let our son go in the front yard to shoot hoops without someone watching him. We didn't want anything to happen to another child in our family.

Was I paranoid? Yes, you could say that, but it's better to be safe than sorry. I have found that many people, particularly parents, were agreeing with me.

Into the third week of Valiree's abduction, I called the news media and the sheriff department for updates everyday.

On Saturday night October 30th, Valiree's case was featured on the television show "America's Most Wanted."

The sheriff's department told me on Monday, that the show generated a few tips, however the investigators had developed no solid leads in Valiree's disappearance.

"We're looking for any break, any evidence in this case."

❀ ❀ ❀

The Move

Brad was spotted moving items out of his home into a storage unit.

When Kathy called me on Saturday, the day after I left Spokane and told me that Brad was spotted loading a truck, boy did thoughts start streaming in.

What in the world could he be moving? Why had he waited for me to leave town before making a move like this? Was he moving Valiree's things? If so, why would he?

I told my sister to stay near his home until I could get Jodel and Steve over to help keep watch. If Brad was moving, I wanted to know. I told her to follow him to see where he was going. I had to know what he was up to.

I thought about Valiree trying to get home. I thought that if somehow she got away and called home, no one would be there.

When Steve and Jodel showed up, they called

me from their cellular phone. They said that Brad had loaded a truck with different items. Some of them looked like they might belong to a child. —*A child like Valiree.*

Steve went on to tell me that the news media was there, too. He handed his phone to one of the reporters from KREM, the CBS affiliate. I told the reporter how I appreciated their continuous coverage.

He assured me that if Brad was moving, they were planning to follow him as far as they were allowed. The reporter was interested in more than a story. It was as if the reporters had made a personal commitment to find Valiree and I appreciated that.

While I was talking to the reporter he quickly handed the phone back to Steve. Steve told me that Brad had gotten into the truck and was pulling off. Steve and Jodel pulled out behind Brad and followed him.

Brad wasn't moving at all, he was only house cleaning. He went to put his things in storage. Although I was somewhat relieved, I was more leery than ever about Brad.

After this incident, I felt the urgency to get back to Spokane ASAP. I had to make sure that the same thing wouldn't happen to Valiree that happened to Roseann.

When I left Spokane in 1992, my sister's case came to a complete halt. As the cold weather and snow came in it appeared that Roseann was forgotten. I wasn't going to let that happen to Valiree.

I sensed something odd happening. I had to get back. It seemed like everything was dying down with Valiree's case. Like mother, like daughter?

I knew that Sheriff Sterk and his staff were working on the evidence they had compiled. However, I also knew that the cold weather would be hitting soon and that they could use all the help they could get to find Valiree.

❀ ❀ ❀

The Vigil

A prayer vigil was coordinated for Valiree on Thursday evening November 4th, at Terrace View Park in the Spokane Valley. It saddened me that I was unable to attend.

I was told how the candles flickered in the night; how the faces of children and adults were lit by their dancing glow, but the occasion was somber.

About 100 people gathered to pray for Valiree's return. Neighbors and friends, strangers and family—all joined to pray together.

The children held their candles tightly, watching the melting wax puddle around the wicks before dripping down one side. Sons and daughters leaned against their daddies and stood close to their mommies. Some parents wrapped their arms around their kids.

It was rather scary to be standing outside, in the dark, thinking about someone you know who was missing. A 9-year-old child was taken in broad daylight, in front of her own home, waiting for her daddy to walk her to school.

Having parents by their side that night made these kids feel safe. Good parents protect their children so no harm comes to them. Children depend on them and trust them to keep them safe. These kids knew they were safe that night.

Together, the children and adults formed a circle of light. Maybe to light the way for Valiree to find her way home safely

A neighbor of the Jacksons said God inspired her to organize the vigil. Other mothers and the pastors in the neighborhood helped her.

Before the prayers started, Captain John Simmons from the Spokane County Sheriff's Department spoke about Valiree's case and their progress.

"The department has put in over 700 hours looking for Valiree and more than 150 tips have been generated from the news and the fliers."

He looked around to see all the people and the flames from their candles.

"We get renewed strength when we see the community respond like this. We're hoping to get a break. Just that one little something that will lead us to Valiree, or what happened to her."

The captain stepped aside and directed the people to Keith Kirkingburg, the Chaplain for the Sheriff's Department. As he was about to offer his words of comfort, the eyes of the many concerned people were fixed on the fire they were holding.

"First, I want to say to the families of Valerie Jackson that all of us walk with them. You are not alone. Secondly, the law enforcement is not giving up on finding Valiree. They're committed to solving this case. And thirdly, there's hardly a day when someone doesn't ask me what they can do to help."

He paused, to keep from choking on his words, "I tell them to pray."

Everyone bowed their head in silence. The candles they were holding seemed to burn stronger—brighter with renewed strength. Then, the soft voices from the children were heard.

"Please come home, Valiree," they whispered.

"Valiree's my best friend. I miss her."

"I feel empty inside. I can't forget you, Valiree."

Then a sixth grader from Valiree's school stepped forward and introduced the 23rd Psalm with these words: "I read this when I'm afraid:

> The Lord is my Shepherd.
> I shall not want.
> In verdant pasture, He gives me repose.
> Beside restful waters, He leads me.
> He refreshes my soul.
> He guides me in right paths for
> His name's sake.
> Although I walk in the dark valley,
> I fear no evil.
> For you are at my side with your rod
> and your staff that give me courage.
> You spread the table before me in
> the sight of my foes.

You anoint my head with oil.
My cup overflows.
Only goodness and kindness follow
me all the days of my life.
I shall dwell in the house of the
Lord for years to come.

A comforting hush fell over the crowd. Eyes filled with tears and souls were somewhat soothed in a quiet way.

Brad, who was present, uttered a few words.

"Everyone's been super. I want to thank everybody. The way the community has come together. Thank you very much."

The crowd was sympathetic for him and his mother. No one could imagine what they were going through. Friends and neighbors comforted Brad's mother as she cried.

"All I want is my granddaughter home."

The candles were blown out and the wax solidified with their burnt wicks. It was dark again. They left Valiree's vigil feeling hopeful.

❀ ❀ ❀

I'm Ba-a-ack

When I arrived back in Phoenix on the 29th of October, I couldn't focus on anything but Valiree. I was still dreaming about my sister. I was in so much pain, physical and emotional. The emotional pain I understood, but I didn't understand the physical pain.

The pain in my face was unbearable. My eye sockets were not just sore, but felt like they were on fire. My ears were aching. My jaw and teeth were tensed. I couldn't stop crying. It was as though I was possessed. I had an urgency about my being that I couldn't control.

I went to my doctor to get checked out. He told me that I was experiencing a high level of tension. He prescribed pain pills for me which I filled as soon as I left his office. That was November 3rd. The pills didn't relieve the pain. I couldn't find any relief.

The next morning, I went to my health club, the Phoenix Fitness. I sat in the sauna, which was set at 185 degrees for almost a half-hour, but the pain in my face was still unbearable. I then got into the jacuzzi which was set at 105 degrees, then my body finally started to relax. Tears started flowing like never before. I was crying— crying publicly. My cries were loud; I was hurting. The pool cleaner was cleaning the pool and jacuzzi. He listened and consoled me. I was angry. I felt that I had let my sister down. I went home after that workout, and took double the recommended dosage of painkillers and slept through the night.

However, when I awoke the next morning, the same excruciating pain had gotten worse. I got dressed and immediately left the house that morning in search of a dentist. I thought that maybe my teeth were the cause.

I stopped by the dental offices that are located within minutes of my home. The receptionist at the front desk rearranged the dentists schedule to accommodate me. Everyone was very understanding. While sitting in the chair waiting for the dentist, I began to cry uncontrollably. They were kind enough to bring me plenty of tissues. I didn't know what was happening to me. After they took X-rays the dentist approached me with the results. He told me that my teeth were in great shape and that there were no infections.

He then asked me if he could get personal with me. I told him, please. He explained to me that I needed to find a way to relax, or my jaw would lock. He said that it was okay if I tell him what was bothering me, so I did.

Again, the tears flowed. After he let me unload, he comforted me with a few words of wisdom. He prescribed a painkiller that was more potent than the one I had. I left the dental office feeling better than when I arrived.

I was receiving phone call after phone call from Spokane. People who I didn't know were calling me to find out when I was coming back to Spokane.

Many of the calls were from women.

They were telling me that things had quieted down since I left. Some were telling me that they were afraid to let their kids play outside. They wanted the person or persons that were responsible for Valiree's abduction to be caught. They wanted Valiree safe and unharmed. They had kids and they were scared.

However, one of those telephone callers didn't want me back. The caller told me to stay out of Spokane. I hung the telephone up and was more determined than ever to get back to Spokane. Finally the time had come for me to go back.

My wife and boys told me to be careful and find Roseann and Valiree. I knew my wife was highly suspicious of Brad and didn't know if he and I would come to blows or not. This worried her, and I knew it. We were one and she couldn't hide her true feelings from me.

When my wife dropped me off at the Phoenix airport our hug was longer than usual. We both believed that Valiree's life was our responsibility now and we couldn't allow fear to creep in, regardless if it cost me my life. Valiree would be found.

Returning to Spokane was an emotional trip. As I flew into Spokane, Tuesday November 9th, on Southwest Airlines, I mapped out my strategy. The mysterious disappearance of Roseann and then seven years later Valiree seemed too coincidental, too bizarre. The weather was getting colder, the snow should be coming soon, and the ground would freeze, just as it had back then. It was eerie.

46

I felt an urgency born of panic and desperation stirring within me. I wanted to find Valiree. My wife and I wanted to adopt her. We wanted her alive. I had to find my sister's baby; I had come to understand the message in my dreams. I felt extremely motivated and determined.

Roseann always gave me strength when we were in school together. She made me feel like I could do anything.

I had criminal negligence on my mind. I figured that Brad could at least be proven guilty of that.

Arriving back in Spokane on the 8:10 PM flight, I was met at the airport by Steve and Jodel with a news reporter from FOX 28 News television.

After the interview with FOX, I told them that I was back to continue the search for Valiree. I picked up my luggage and Steve and Jodel drove me to the Quality Inn in the Spokane Valley.

I checked in and went to my room. Alone and with too much time to think— too much time to think about what might have happened to Valiree and how her life may have been. I wondered if Valiree had been able to live a normal child's life, or if she had lived in fear. I was trying to piece things together. I had to do something— something to draw the guilty party out. Someone had to know where Valiree was.

I knew there were people still distributing fliers and still very concerned. They had somewhat continued what we had been doing a few weeks ago. The effort needed a shot in the arm. There was a need here to do something different.

Out of this desire arose the decision to start a paper that would list pictures of abused, missing and exploited children. My mission would be to expose to the world how to protect children and women in all communities. Their vulnerability would become their strength.

The paper was to be named "The Exposure." My appeal to the community and the world would be to make criminals accountable by exposing their victims, exposing what the criminals did to the children and women whom they assaulted and exposing the criminals themselves.

Crimes against humanity should be subjected to public ridicule and scorn. They must be met with the severest punishment that the law will allow.

❁ ❁ ❁

Getting the Word Out Again

As an advertising executive for the past 15 years, I knew what it took to get the word out. I knew that the media was important, especially in this situation. More coverage and exposure from the media would work in Valiree's favor, I was sure about that.

Mike Quiggle, whose married to my aunt Roberta, had been working with me for the past six months. We had recently completed a paper that covered the opening of Safeco Field, the new baseball stadium for the Seattle Mariners. The paper was a success.

Mike and I understood how a paper splattered with Valiree's picture on it could be instrumental in her recovery. We were both determined to get things started. Mike had an edge on me when it came to the criminal mind. He had worked for the Washington State Correctional Department for the past 27 years.

Mike and Roberta were devastated when they heard the news about Valiree. They called and told me that they were heading to Spokane from their home in Shelton, Washington. I told them that I would take care of the hotel accommodations and meet with them upon their arrival.

I called the Fairfield Inn in Spokane and spoke to Kimberly, the manager of the hotel. I explained to her that I was Valiree's uncle and that I would be arriving in Spokane on Tuesday, November 9th. I told her that I needed to reserve two rooms because I would be having guests. Kimberly was more than generous. She told me that the rooms would be waiting for me upon my arrival.

After hanging up with Kimberly, I started to think about all of us staying at the same hotel and that bothered me. I picked up the phone and called another one of my favorite hotels.

While in the advertising business for years, Spokane was part of my territory. My oldest son went to high school there while living with his mother Jodel, my former wife and her husband Steve. Besides being raised in Spokane, I have family and friends that always make my stay enjoyable.

The Spokane Valley Quality Inn was just that, quality. I had come to enjoy their accommodations as well as their hospitality. When I called the hotel, the general manager Mike Lupo expressed his feelings concerning Valiree. He and his sales director Connie Wagner told me that they would do anything to help find Valiree and that that included putting me up. I thanked them and told them that I would be there on Tuesday. Mike and Roberta were also arriving the same day.

Wednesday morning Mike, Roberta and I got together in their room at the Fairfield Inn. When I arrived, the person at the front desk recognized me right away. She told me that the Quiggles were in my room. They were anxious to get started on finding Valiree. I was pleasantly surprised. I was finding out just how wonderful and caring people in Spokane were. This was a perfect example.

Mike and Roberta were already hard at work when I got to their room.

"Let's get out there and find Valiree— just maybe we'll get lucky and find Roseann as well."

He sent a charge right into me. We made plans and discussed our strategy concerning the paper. We worked out the layout, contracts, business cards, and other paperwork necessary to get this project moving quickly.

After finishing our plans, I phoned Brad. A woman answered. She might have been one of his girlfriends or his mother. She didn't identify herself, but she knew who I was. She sounded surprised to hear that I was back in Spokane again.

"I need to talk with Brad. We need to work together on this situation to find Valiree. Could you have him call me?" I gave her my number.

"You bet, you bet. I'll make sure he calls you."

The conversation ended with that and I hung up.

We needed more fliers to distribute. I called National Color Graphics, a Spokane printer and talked with the owner. I asked if he would print some fliers with Valiree's picture on them. He agreed. He was great.

He told me that he would consider it an honor to help find Valiree. Not only did National Color print the fliers, but they donated them as well. They printed 5,000 full-colored fliers. Their help was truly appreciated.

Once we had the fliers, Mike and I started passing them out while promoting the new paper.

While Mike and I were distributing the fliers, Roberta was phoning business owners in hopes of getting their involvement. Her presentation was mixed with many tears. She found it hard to get through a conversation without thinking about Valiree and her niece Roseann. Mike was no different and neither was I. We were all emotional wrecks, but that didn't stop us. We were determined to get the word out, regardless of how we felt.

We went to Riverpark Square, the South Hill, and the North Side businesses. The big grocery store chains were great. Safeway, Tidyman's, Rosauers, Yoke's— all gladly participated. Tidyman's even placed the fliers directly in the grocery bags. Wal-Mart and Kmart were also supportive. They were more than willing to participate. The cooperative effort to find Valiree was very moving.

The interviews and coverage continued, not only on local TV stations, but regional and national stations were starting to pay attention, too. The radio was keeping hourly updates.

That night I went to bed exhausted. The pain in my face was getting worse.

I wasn't able to sleep with the voice inside my head crying all night. There were times that being alone in my room got real scary. I didn't sleep well at all. The dreams were more persistent than ever, they had become so real. "Find my baby, find my baby!"

I got on my knees and prayed for understanding. What in the heck was happening to me? It was as if I was trapped in my dreams and couldn't get out. My sister's voice kept echoing through my mind. She sounded so desperate. Then the morning came.

❀ ❀ ❀

The Call

"Hello, John. This is Brad Jackson."

I was shocked to hear Brad's voice. I thought he was going to tell me to stop driving by his house.

I had been driving by Brad's house periodically since my arrival. I was only keeping an eye on things. I knew that he knew I was out there. He peered out the window on a couple of my drive-bys, but he didn't call me until the morning of November 11th.

"Are you shocked I'm calling?"

Of course I was shocked and he knew it. Brad never in his life ever bothered to call me. He knew we had been looking for him and Valiree for the past seven years.

It was 9:00 Thursday morning. I wondered briefly how he knew to contact me there and not at the Fairfield. I was suspicious of what he was up to.

"John, I really appreciate what you're doing. I know that you love Valiree and I appreciate what you're doing. I don't understand why everyone is so upset over this situation with Valiree."

I was shocked to hear him say that. What could he possibly mean? His daughter was MISSING!

"It's none of their business! It's only our business and I wish they would stop doing what they're doing! I wish you would stop the media and stop the press and stop everything else! All this coverage is unnecessary! The police are stupid! They don't even know what they are doing! They couldn't find Roseann and won't find Valiree, because she's going to come home."

I sensed a tinge of anger.

"Roseann never had this kind of coverage when she disappeared! There just wasn't all this fuss back then!"

He spoke in a tone laced with irritation.

"Why are you doing all this? We don't need anyone else!"

Did he think everything would be the same with Valiree's disappearance as it was with Roseann's— like mother, like daughter? I let him talk.

"I have one of the fliers that you're putting out describing your new paper. You really don't need to be doing that, you know.

I'll tell ya, man, she's coming home. I really don't understand why all this coverage is going on."

Who did he think he was kidding? An innocent, grief-stricken father would do anything possible to find his missing child. He certainly would not do anything to prevent the action that might lead to her recovery. Was he sick or something?

"What are you putting in the paper? What's it all about and what's the Fairfield Inn got to do with it?"

The fliers that Mike and I were passing out had the Fairfield Inn printed on them along with my name and room number.

I told him that safety tips and pictures of kids who were missing would be in it, particularly, Valiree. The paper was for Valiree and her mother. I wanted to find them and for now, this was the best way that I could think of. I went on to tell him that the Fairfield Inn was interested in Valiree's safe recovery as well.

"Are you putting anything in it about me?"

Ah-ha, the reason for the call.

I told him that at that time, no.

Why should I? I hadn't convicted him. He hadn't done anything, had he? Why should he be in the paper?

"Oh, good. You're sure there's nothing in there about me? I was just wondering— I can trust you then?"

My suspicions were justified. Brad was calling about himself. I had him worried. He didn't sound like he was worried about Valiree and that frightened me.

"Yes, you can trust me Brad."

That's exactly what I wanted. I wanted his trust. I wanted him to call me and he did. I knew that he really didn't want to talk me, but I was a puzzlement to him and he was trying to figure me out.

"John, we need to get together sometime. My parents and I would like to have you over for dinner. How about this Saturday?"

I accepted. However, in two days, on Saturday, I found out, that it wouldn't be for dinner.

The Sheriff's Chaplain, Keith Kirkingburg, called me shortly after Brad and I finished our conversation. He confirmed my dinner plans with Brad and his family. He told me that Brad believed that I was telling the media that he was involved in Valiree's abduction. He thought it was about time that Brad and I work together to find her. Although Brad was my number one suspect, I agreed with him that we should work together and have dinner together on Saturday.

❀ ❀ ❀

Adding to the List

On Thursday and Friday, November 11th and 12th, my uncle and I continued passing out fliers and promoting my paper. I continued giving interviews with the media as well.

The word about Valiree was getting out and I was becoming a familiar face, thanks to the media. Whether I was walking on the street, eating in a restaurant or entering a business, people would stop me.

"John! You're John Stone, I've seen you on TV."

I would get encouragement from people to keep looking for Valiree. They wanted Valiree found. They were parents too, and were scared for their sons and daughters. They wanted to let their kids go out to play, but too much was going on in their town. Not only was there too much going on, but too many children were being murdered in Spokane and their parents were being accused of killing them.

There was Debra Eik, who drove her dark green Yukon sport utility vehicle to a secluded road in Spokane Valley. She was accused of shooting Brandon and Brian, her two sons, with a .38-caliber handgun.

There was Robert Wood, who was accused of strangling Christopher, his 11-year-old son, and stuffing him in a garbage can. The father claimed the boy set their Liberty Lake house on fire then ran away. Before he could be tried, he committed suicide.

There was Sharon Curry, who is accused of stabbing Jessica, her 8- year-old daughter to death while sitting in a parked car in their driveway in Medical Lake. She is also accused of stabbing herself.

Spokane was my home. It saddened me to hear about so many children being murdered or abused in my old stomping ground. I was more determined than ever to find Valiree in spite of the cost. Brad knew this.

I called Sheriff Sterk and set up a meeting to discuss Brad's unanticipated phone call to me. Mike and I went to the Public Safety Building and met with the Sheriff and Lieutenant Silver in one of their offices. They were both anxious to hear about the phone call from Brad. Lieutenant Silver grabbed a notepad and began writing.

Sheriff Sterk wanted details. He asked me to try to recall the phone conversation with Brad, word for word. After my detailed description, they looked perplexed.

"Brad told us that he would never call you. John, I need to know what you think Brad is up to." He was not cooperating with them in any way.

I told them that Brad had invited me to dinner and that I was planning on attending. I thought Brad was playing games, but my number-one priority was to find Valiree and if that meant having dinner with Brad, then I was going to do just that.

They were concerned. They told me to make an effort to remember everything that Brad and I talk about during dinner.

Mike was concerned about my safety, too. He didn't think it was a good idea going to Brad's house alone. He asked them about deputizing me. Sheriff Sterk said that if they deputized me, then I would have to inform Brad of that fact. My hands would be tied and Brad wouldn't want to talk to me.

I saw the logic and agreed that I should not be deputized. I knew what had to be done and I was willing to do it.

Upon leaving, Sheriff Sterk and I shook hands. With a sincere look in his eyes, he told me to be careful and promised that he wouldn't give up on Valiree.

Mike and I went to the streets again. I felt as if I had found a new friend. It felt good knowing that he along with Lieutenant Silver, Captain Simmons, Sergeant Goodwin and the rest of their department were working on Valiree's case.

❀ ❀ ❀

Shelly's Suspicions

After returning to my room in the evenings, I consistently had many phone messages waiting for me. I returned most of them. I figured that maybe, just maybe, one of those calls could lead me to my sister and Valiree.

One call was from Shelly Egeland. Shelly was the nearby neighbor of the Jacksons who lived two and a half blocks away. She was the one who spent the day with Brad and his mother shortly after Valiree's disappearance.

Shelly said that she had a lot of information and wanted to talk to me. She hadn't called earlier because she didn't know how Brad and his parents would feel about it. For some reason some people in Spokane doubted my sincerity.

She thought that I had all the information that she had given the sheriff. I encouraged her to tell me what she had told them.

She told me that Brad was constantly bothering her since Valiree's disappearance and that she was becoming increasingly suspicious of him. She was concerned about his actions and reaction to Valiree's abduction.

She said that Jan, the principal at Valiree's

school, told everyone that Brad was a good father and that the school should be supportive of him. The administrators and teachers were very familiar with him. He would go to the school quite often to have lunch with Valiree. Shelly now wondered about the "good father" and began to have suspicions about his frequent school visits.

She recounted how Brad cursed the sheriff and media who were waiting outside his parents' home the day of Valiree's disappearance. She talked about how Brad had pictures of Valiree, but wouldn't give one to the media for hours.

"Why wouldn't he give them a picture of his daughter?"

She told me that she didn't know what Brad was up to and questioned his actions. She was scared for Valiree.

"Brad paced back and forth in the house. He was worried about how the police might be accusing him and wanted them to go away."

Karen, Brad's mother, seemed genuinely upset through the whole ordeal. There was an instance when Karen was manhandled by Brad to "straighten up."

"Then he turned around and looked at me saying, even if the police do suspect me, I'm sticking to my story. He sang the words, 'It's my story and I'm sticking to it', with a weird smile on his face. I felt that was strange, but thought nothing of it until later."

"Brad had Valiree on 20 milligrams of Paxil, an antidepressant. I know some women who are over 200 pounds and were taking 20 milligrams of Paxil.

That was too strong for them. Why would a 70-pound, third grader be prescribed Paxil? I went to the bathroom and saw the prescription bottle of Paxil with Valiree's name on it. I even read a note reminding Valiree to take her pill before going to school."

That was the first time I had heard about Paxil.

Shelly was flabbergasted and very upset about the whole ordeal concerning Valiree. I began to see how my theory of Brad's negligence could be valid. He wasn't acting as a parent should act, regardless of an abduction. The abduction just made his negligence look worse.

Since school was almost out, Shelly told Brad and his mom that she had to get back to help at the crosswalks. Karen asked Shelly to come back and check on them later. After leaving, she had more concerns and discomforts than when she first arrived.

Shelly returned later that evening, around six. She was anxious to know if Brad had heard from Valiree. She was there for about thirty minutes. Before she left, she walked into Karen's bedroom to say goodbye to Brad. He was in there talking to a woman on the phone. Before he turned and said "Hi, Shelly," she heard him say, "My past is finally catching up to me."

She thought later, that the comment she heard might have some significance.

I arranged to get together with her on Saturday morning. I wanted to see if there was anything else that she could tell me to help solve Valiree's puzzle.

❋ ❋ ❋

Plenty of Evidence

I arrived at Shelly's home at 10:00 in the morning on Saturday, November 13th. She introduced me to her husband Kevin and their two children, one of whom had been tutored in math by Valiree.

As we were getting acquainted in their living room, her in-laws Molly and Bob Egeland, Kevin's parents, joined us. Molly and Bob live a few houses down the street from the Jacksons'.

We started talking about Valiree and went over Brad's actions after he announced her abduction. They talked a lot about Valiree and how smart she was. It was evident that she was loved throughout the community.

We all wanted to know why Valiree was on an antidepressant. Had Brad informed the counselor or nurse at school about the Paxil and the bloody noses?

Valiree had dreams and nightmares of her mother as a monster trying to take her away. Did anyone other than Brad know about this? Was Valiree told anything about her mother? What did she really know? By this time there wasn't a dry eye in the house.

"Oh, my God, Brad's guilty! John, what can we do to find Valiree? I pray to God she's still alive!"

We were all trying to figure out what we could do to find Valiree when the phone rang.

❃ ❃ ❃

We Found Something

R-r-r-ring.

It was a call from KXLY.

"The sheriff's digging out on Dishman-Mica Road, Highway 27, in a wooded area. Thought you'd like to know."

We jumped to our feet all at once and ran for our cars. I followed behind, driving alone wondering what this all meant.

I drove at a distance behind the Egelands' because I didn't want Brad to see us together. I was invited to have dinner with him in a few hours and I didn't want to ruin that.

As I was driving to the location, I was thinking about my childhood days in Spokane. There were miles and miles of woods. As a child, I felt safe growing up in Spokane. Sure, we had our share of problems. However, for the most part, we seemed to be sheltered from violence. It's different now. I felt sorry for the children growing up today— not just in Spokane, but everywhere.

Children are our lifeline and I believe that any person who murders a child should be executed.

As my thoughts continued, I started to cry. Tears of sadness and anger were flowing from my eyes. Surely the sheriff's department is looking for someone else, not Valiree.

When I arrived at the location, I had difficulty bringing myself to face the reality that they were actually digging to find Valiree's body. I stopped short of the site, just around the corner, and got out of my car. I hiked up the hill to pull myself together. I took several deep breaths to try to calm down.

I did not want to face the reality that they might find her body. I did not want to accept that Valiree was dead. Consequently, there I was, possibly having to accept the ill fate of my sister as well. I refused to believe that. I kept telling myself—Roseann is alive and Valiree is with her, that's what I'll believe.

I convinced myself that this was a wild goose chase. I got back into my car and repeated the same words over and over again.

"They won't find her, they won't find her—she's still alive. She has to be."

I drove down into the gully where the trees seem to go on for miles where the digging was occurring. As soon as I pulled up, I walked up to Captain Simmons.

"There's nothing here, right?"

I was trying to hold back my emotions. I wanted to appear strong, to keep the faith that Valiree was still alive.

"You definitely have not found anything, right? There's no way that you found anything, right?"

As I spoke, a panic crept into my voice and a feeling of nausea started moving through my gut. He looked at me sympathetically.

"We found something John and it's leading us to believe that it belongs to Valiree."

As I put my hands on Captain Simmons shoulders and slumped down, he caught me. I felt like a huge boulder had fallen on my chest. It hurt so bad. The pain, the despair, I couldn't handle it. Captain Simmons consoled me like a friend. He told me that he was there for me day or night.

Even though I felt awful, I stayed around the next four hours until 3:00pm, scouring the woods above the site, looking for loose ground, prodding and walking through brush and branches. I was hoping and praying that Valiree wasn't there. Saturday passed, still no Valiree— still no Roseann.

As I was walking back toward my car, I managed to give a statement to the television reporters. I wanted to make it very clear that I was going after Brad for negligence. Looking at the TV cameras, I declared emphatically:

"Brad Jackson is guilty of negligence, guilty of criminal negligence! I will not stop until he is behind bars! I will never give up until Brad Jackson is behind bars and if he has done something to hurt Valiree, I will not give up on that either!"

For a moment, I had forgotten about my dinner plans with Brad. Immediately after I said those words, I knew for sure that our dinner plans would be canceled. I was enraged. The point that I was trying to make was that I was going after Brad for his negligence.

I left Dishman-Mica feeling better than when I had arrived. At least they hadn't found Valiree's body. I continued to hope that she was still alive.

❀ ❀ ❀

The Shotgun

After I left the Dishman Mica site on Saturday, I drove back slowly to my room at the Quality Inn. I arrived back at the hotel around 5:00. I tried to stay positive because no body had been found. My spirits sank considerably with the realization that they were in fact looking for a body, Valiree's body.

The phone was ringing as I stepped in. I answered it quickly, hoping for some good news.

"John, the sheriff is impounding Brad's truck at his house. KHQ and KREM are out at the scene."

I called and I asked Steve and Jodel to drive over to Brad's and check it out. I didn't think that I should be seen over there, especially since I had just stated on television that my intentions were to put Brad behind bars for negligence.

They called back a little while later and said that they saw Brad's truck being towed away. This was the second time. Three weeks prior to this incident, his truck had been towed away by the sheriff, but had been returned to Brad at the beginning of that week.

Why were they so interested in his truck again?

Another phone call informed me that the sheriff was now looking for Brad. They knew he was driving around with a shotgun in his car.

I knew for certain that our dinner plans were canceled then.

I got a call from KREM TV news reporter Jeff Humphrey.

"John, Brad's got a shotgun. Are you safe?"

I told Jeff that I had fastened the locks on my door. He said to be careful and that he'd keep me informed of Brad's whereabouts.

Oh, Lord, I know Brad is heading my way.

At first I thought that my pressuring him was about to cost me my life. Jeff Humphrey heard the desperation in my voice.

"John are you sure you're alright?"

He told me not to panic and again said that he would keep me updated. I appreciated the fact that he had become more than just a reporter. He had my back, but my front was wide open. I had been playing with Brad's emotions since my first arrival in Spokane.

Inside my room, I secured all three locks on the door. I even double-checked them after Humphrey's phone call.

Then I moved over to the windows, looked out, and pop the screen out of one. I eyed the distance from the window to the ground and was dismayed to see that I couldn't jump out safely. However, if I had to exit quickly, that would be the only way to go.

I needed to make my descent more safe so I threw the bedspread and blanket off my bed and pulled the sheets off. I tied them together quickly, tugging and pulling to make sure the knots would hold. If I had to go out the window, I wanted the sheets to support my fast getaway with little or no injury to myself.

If Brad showed up with a shotgun, I guessed that the locks on the hotel door needed two shotgun blasts to get in. With the second blast, I hoped that I would be out the window, on the ground, and running for my life.

I sat in my room answering the phone, waiting for that knock to come blasting at my door. The telephone kept ringing from one source after another, telling me how everyone was trying to find Brad.

Although I called home every night to update my family, I felt an urgency now more than ever to talk to them. However, one of my teenage sons had the phone tied up.

During a conversation with Shelly that night, I mentioned that I couldn't get through to my family. I told her to make sure she let them know if anything happened to me.

I just stayed in my room, waiting. Waiting for who knows what. I kept checking the knots in the sheets, considered the distance from my window to the ground, and where I would run.

Several hours passed. It seemed like an eternity. Then, I got another call from Jeff Humphrey.

"John, they just picked Brad up downtown with the shotgun.

They're taking him to the psychiatric ward at Sacred Heart Hospital."

"They picked him up where, downtown?"

"In the Perkin's parking lot."

Oh, Lord, that's the Fairfield Inn's parking lot, too.

The Perkin's Restaurant and the Fairfield Inn share the same parking lot. Brad must have thought I was staying at the Fairfield Inn. He was parked six spaces from the window of what would have been my room. He was looking for me at the wrong place. I'm not sure how that happened.

Although Brad had called me at the Quality Inn, he obviously didn't know that I was staying there. On the other hand, he simply did not make the connection between the phone number and the hotel. The flier Brad had obtained describing my paper had the Fairfield Inn's phone and room number on it. At the bottom of the flier was my signature.

What was he was thinking? He made the wrong choice between Quality Inn and Fairfield Inn and apparently was confused about where I was staying. I was thankful for that.

Being close to midnight, I wanted to make sure that Brad was admitted to the hospital. If he was not there, I knew that I would be up all night, looking at my door with its three locks, checking my knotted sheets, and repeating the best escape routes in my head. I needed to see for myself that Brad was apprehended so I could get some sleep.

Jodel and Steve were wonderful. Steve was always telling me to be careful.

He knew I was suspicious of Brad from the very beginning. They came by and together we drove to the hospital to confirm that Brad was there. He was admitted for suicide watch. We were happy to see that he was in fact there. However, no tests could be run until the staff was available. Since it was about midnight, I knew that he would be there for at least the next 48 hours before he would be released.

I returned to my room hoping to get some sleep. I couldn't sleep. I was thinking about what could happen next. I was trying to piece things together: the conversation I had with Brad on Thursday, the Sheriff taking his truck again, Brad having a shotgun, parking outside my room at the Fairfield Inn, and going berserk.

Was he going to plead insanity? Did he commit himself to psychiatric care maintaining he couldn't handle Valiree being missing? Is that why he wasn't at the site today?

I didn't know where this was going. I had absolutely no doubt as to Brad's guilt, but I didn't know how he was trying to set himself up to look. I still wasn't sure what he had done to Valiree. I prayed she was still alive.

I had very little sleep that night, wondering and worrying what was going to happen next. I knew I had to be ready.

Another Goose Chase

I tried to get some sleep but failed. It was Sunday morning and I was beat. I thought about going to Calvary Baptist Church to worship with friends, but I had to go back out and look for Valiree.

Mike and Roberta came to my room and we drove over to Shelly and Kevin Egeland's house. Kevin's parents, Molly, Bob along with his brother, Scott, met us there. All eight of us talked in their living room and tried piecing things together. We asked many questions among ourselves.

What did Brad do with Valiree? Did he owe money to a drug dealer and had to hide her so she wouldn't get hurt? Did he sell her to a pornography or prostitution ring? Did he drug her, so when she returned she wouldn't know where she was? Why did the sheriff take Brad's truck again? Where was Valiree?

None of us wanted to believe that Valiree could be dead. Everyone started crying.

Not having answers to any of our questions, we decided to go back out to the Dishman digging site, hoping something would turn up.

When we arrived, we were shocked to find that no one was there— I mean no one. We drove around a little more and still didn't find any activity. Curious about what was going on, we used Mike's cell phone to call the KXLY news station for an update.

"Oh, they're looking in a new area northwest of Spokane in Stevens County, close to Springdale, Washington, about 50-60 miles from where you guys are now. A hunter tipped off the Sheriff. They're up there today, doing some looking and digging off an old logging road."

We hurried onto the highway, going 60, 70, 80 miles an hour and arrived around 2:00. The news crew and searchers were already there.

After a few inquires, I discovered that the Sheriff had reason to believe Valiree's body was somewhere at this site.

"How do you know? What makes you think that? When did you learn of this? Who told you? Why do you believe she's out here?"

One anxious question followed another.

I thought Brad was saying things in the psychiatric ward to lead these people on a wild-goose chase. It just had to be another wild goose chase, like yesterday. I didn't want to believe what thcy wcrc suggesting was true.

We waited until dusk. The sheriff approached me again. His eyes were so expressive. I respected him and appreciated his department's hard work.

"There's nothing right now. We'll be back tomorrow. We'll have something for you by noon. Go home and get some sleep."

In my heart, I still clung to the hope that Valiree was alive.

❀ ❀ ❀

Reflections

My heart was so heavy that Sunday night. It was hard to believe that I was really experiencing all this. It was too horrifying. Maybe this was all just a bad dream. I sat catatonic in my room.

Was Valiree's innocence taken along with her life?

I couldn't eat. My favorite snack was nachos with hot sauce from Casa de Oro Mexican restaurant. The snack sat untouched on the table. I tried to force myself to watch TV to take my mind off things for a while, but found that I couldn't. Every time I closed my eyes, thoughts of my little niece invaded my mind making sleep impossible. I was completely preoccupied with Valiree. I cried and cried. Maybe 10 or 15 different times throughout the night. I cried like never before. I had no control over what I was feeling.

I kept hearing my sister's words echoing in my head, *"Find my baby, find my baby, find my baby!"*

The pain in my face was getting worse as flashbacks of Roseann seized my soul. You see, Roseann and I enjoyed being together and knew each other well. We were in the same grade and sometimes the same classes. Her grades were always better than mine were, but she would encourage me to do better because she knew I could.

Now, I was feeling guilty for not finding her in 1992. I should have listened to my mom and put more pressure on the police to thoroughly investigate Roseann's disappearance. 1 knew I could have done a better job, just like getting those better grades. I felt hopeless.

As I envisioned her most beautiful smile, she was so real and alive that night. I could feel her right there in the room with me. The tears kept flowing. I was hurting so much.

When I got up to get more tissue, passing by the mirror, the reflection startled me. I stopped and looked more closely. I stepped backward then forward, looking harder at what I saw. I could not believe my eyes.

In the mirror, I didn't see myself at all. All I saw was Roseann. It was as if she was reaching to touch the glass. I placed my fingertips on the mirror trying to touch hers. We had joined. It was as if she was me and I was her. It was eerie but, I understood.

Together, we would find Valiree.

$$\text{❀ ❀ ❀}$$

Day of Discovery

I woke up Monday morning, November 15th, having had very little sleep.

The Sheriff told me they wouldn't know anything until noon. Maybe he said that so I would get some rest, but I couldn't sleep. I had to get out there anyway, as soon as possible, just in case.

By 8:00 I had filled the car with gas and had grabbed a yogurt for breakfast. It was all my stomach could handle. I was too upset.

I knew that if they found Valiree's body, there was a good chance that Brad did something to Roseann as well. That would be too much to digest. I felt my stomach churn and turn because of anticipation and anxiety.

I had been able to keep my sister alive in my memories for the past seven years. I wasn't ready to except her being dead.

I would give anything for some of her Lisa Douglas pancakes.

I headed out to the site where the Sheriff said he would meet me. I didn't know what to expect. It took more time than usual to get there because I cried most of the way.

When I found myself swerving back and forth on the highway because of my blinding tears, I promptly put my blinker on and pulled off to the side of the road. Several times that happened and I had to compose myself before driving any farther. The box of tissue I had just opened was almost empty.

I arrived in Springdale where they were digging around 9:30. The news reporters were there and saw that I was an emotional mess. They shook my hand and left me alone. I appreciated that I wasn't asked for a comment.

I headed toward the Search and Rescue Team. They were working out of a large motor home that had been converted into a command post. I spoke with some of the volunteers. They were great. They tried to distract me from what was going on. They saw my tears as I kept looking up at the hill where the search was going on.

A sheriff's car was blocking the road, monitoring the arrival and departure of cars and people. I watched as vehicles drove in and out, wishing that they would all go away. I wanted everybody off that hill. How I wanted everybody to leave.

I didn't want to believe that there might be a body up there. If I could have pulled everyone off, I would have done it. I didn't want to believe that Valiree was up there. Not Valiree, not my baby. However, I couldn't stop them. I felt so helpless.

God, please help me!

That day, I wore a tie with a painted cross on it. I decided that if they found Valiree or Roseann up there, I was going to lay my tie over the body and pray. My hoped was that they would rise as Lazarus did when he had been dead for several days.

76

Jesus said, as written in the gospel of Saint John, chapter 11, verse 39, "Take away the stone." He also asked, "Did I not tell you that if you believed, you would see the glory of God?" Lazarus walked right out of that cave, which was his burial site.

I believed then and still do that with God, all things are possible. My faith and trust in my heavenly father was only being strengthened. I am so thankful, because he does hear us and he has always— and I do mean always— comes through. I believe we might not understand God's purpose, but it doesn't matter because God understands what's best for us.

Lord, Jesus, give me strength.

I felt Roseann's presence. I could hear her crying, "Find my baby, find my baby." I turned toward the hill and prayed. My head throbbed with each heartbeat. My chest felt tight with pain. It was so hard to just be there and simply wait for the news.

I started pacing back and forth— I so was restless. I was hoping this was just another game Brad was playing and that Valiree was still alive. This was torture. I knew that I had to keep pushing— pushing to find the truth.

Official-looking cars kept driving up. When they did, I would hurry toward them asking why they were there and what did they want. All I got were general routine answers.

Then I watched a white Porsche drive up and stop. A man in a blue smock with short sleeves stepped out. I ran over to him.

"Who are you?" I asked anxiously, afraid of what he might say but, needed to know. He told me he was the forensic doctor.

"W-w-what are you doing here? What's a forensic person doing here anyway? There's nothing up there for you to be here for."

My blood shot eyes and whole body turned toward the hill.

"I know, I know," he calmly replied. "But sometimes we come out on investigations just to see if there's something here that we can help with."

A forensic doctor, 60 miles from town, in a short-sleeved shirt on a cold day in November like he's in a hurry to get here, just taking a Monday afternoon drive? Did he have nothing better to do? Who are they kidding? What have they found up on that hill?

At that point, a sharp stab of pain suddenly shot through my body. I sucked in my breath and closed my swollen eyes afraid to think about anything.

I didn't want to believe it. I closed it off, boy did I close it off.

Next thing I knew, the coroner came. Oh, Lord, did my mind start to go. I did the same thing I did with the forensic person.

I asked the same questions and got the same answers. Apparently, the coroner had read from the same script has the forensic doctor.

My heart grew faint. I was feeling weaker and weaker by the moment. I was still desperately holding on to the thought that they weren't finding anything, that maybe it was just a dead animal they were looking at, or it was someone else up there. Not that I wanted anyone to be buried up there either. I didn't want any body to be up there.

Please, God, not Valiree. Least of all, not Valiree. Not Roseann.

I started pacing faster and franticly, back and forth. I couldn't stop.

The news reporters were so understanding. They gave me all the space and time I needed throughout the entire ordeal to get my thoughts together. They didn't crowd me looking for a story. This ordeal had been hard for them to handle too.

Shortly after three o' clock, I watched as Sheriff Sterk come down the hill from where they had been searching. His face was sullen as his eyes shifted from me, to the media crews, then back to me again.

"I need to talk with the family first."

When he said that, my knees buckled.

I knew something was seriously wrong. I couldn't hide from it anymore.

Lord, have mercy.

My heart was racing as the Sheriff quietly muttered the words of horror I dreaded hearing.

"We have found what we believe to be Valiree's body."

All I can remember in those next few moments was going off to the side, hitting the ground.

As I sat on the ground, Mike, Roberta, and Steve came over to comfort me. I cried on Jodel's shoulder. We were all spent. They were as upset as I was. Sheriff Sterk's eyes were bloodshot. He couldn't hide his hurt from me. He whispered a few words of comfort to me and headed over to the press.

At that moment, I no longer wanted to be on this earth. I didn't want to be a part of all the madness. I wanted to be with Valiree. I wanted to be with her mom. I couldn't— I mustn't, but that's just how I felt.

Steve and Mike, with one of Steve's friends, helped me over to my car. The news reporters were gracious. They saw my condition and allowed me to leave the scene without pressuring me for a story.

I got in the back seat of my rental car and Steve drove my car with Jodel, while Steve's friend drove theirs. Mike and Roberta got into their car and led us away from the scene.

❃ ❃ ❃

Turning Around

We got about a mile down the road and I realized what had happened.

Wait a minute, people. Just wait a minute.

In an instant, I began to see things from a different perspective. I couldn't allow Darkness to believe that there was a victory here. I had to tell the public about this. I had to let people know. I had to stand strong and let the world know that Valiree Jackson stands for something.

Valiree Jackson stands for the reason that some kind of legislation needs to be passed to deal with people who think they can get away with murder. Valiree Jackson is the reason to put child killers of the world to death.

I didn't want Valiree's death to be in vain. All her pain, all her suffering, it just can't be in vain. Through her, we can help. We need to make communities become more aware. We need to fill the cracks so children and women out there don't fall through them.

Taking the life of a child, an innocent dependent, is the worst crime against an individual, a family, a community, and the world. It is the worst crime against all natural law; all man made laws, and divine law.

The tragic life and death of Valiree Jackson at the hands of a child killer had to be turned around into a way to stop others from doing this sort of thing. We cannot allow what happened to Valiree to ever happen again— never again, ever! So help us, God.

As I left the gravesite at Stevens County, I felt weak. The farther we drove, the weaker I became. Then all of the sudden it was as though someone had picked me up. I felt as though my sister was with me. Roseann was with me.

"Let's turn around. Please let's go back and make a difference."

As we drove back, I could feel myself getting stronger and stronger. A strength to make changes. The strength to inform, educate, and assist people in order to stop sub-humans.

To stop them from committing the worst imaginable crimes against life.

My quest was to allow Valiree to live on in everyone else's life. Her life was not to be wasted and I vowed to my Creator that it would not go to waste.

In my heart and soul, the Valiree Jackson Bill was born that day, the day her body was discovered in a shallow hole that her killer dug.

I had Steve stop the car. I went back to the gravesite and I asked to see Valiree's body.

"John, you don't want to see her right now," the sheriff responded.

Sheriff Sterk knew it wasn't a pretty sight. It was hard for him and his crew to see Valiree's body. A little girl like their daughters, their nieces, their neighbors. It was hard for them to do what they had to do. The sheriff wanted to spare me from any more grief for the time being. The body of a loved one who had been dead for four weeks was not something anyone should have to see. Especially not that of a child.

"Listen, we'll be doing an autopsy and then we'll get her ready for you to see tomorrow. It's better that way."

I listened and didn't insist on looking at Valiree, lying there in the place where dirt, sticks, and rocks surrounded her. She was left dead in a plastic bag to rot like a piece of meat.

I accepted not seeing her then. I had to build strength. Strength to see her on Tuesday. I had to see her. I just had to. I had to follow through with this completely. I owed it to my mom and to my sister. A granddaughter dead. A daughter dead.

If my sister and mom were here they would have been doing what I was doing. I have to see this through for Valiree and for them.

God, help me. In the name of Jesus Christ, help me be strong.

After Valiree's body was found, Sheriff Sterk announced that Brad Jackson was the suspect. They had good reason to believe that Brad had moved Valiree's body from the Dishman-Mica location where they were digging on Saturday, to where the dogs finally found her body.

The thought of that angered me. Then I found out that they suspected that Brad had actually moved her corpse on Friday, November 12th which was the night before our supposed dinner engagement.

It was getting dark and I was finally ready to give a statement to the reporters. The television reporters, Gary Darigold from KHQ, Trova Hutchins from KXLY, Jeff Humphrey from KREM and Kirsten Joyce from Fox 28 News had been at the site all day. I couldn't let them down. Although the day's events brought tears to their eyes, they had a job to do and I was glad they were there. After my statements to the reporters, Steve, Jodel, and I headed back to town.

❋ ❋ ❋

Murder or Murders?

After discovering the freshly dug earth, the sheriff's staff used a Cadaver dog that found the shallow grave where Valiree's corpse lay. A grave not quite two feet deep.

Detectives from the serial killer task force were on the scene at the Stevens County location. Valiree's mother, Roseann, who disappeared in 1992, had been considered a possible serial killer victim.

The Serial Killer Task Force was made up of four county officers, four city officers, and two sergeants. They had compiled over 1000 pieces of evidence against the serial killer. However, this was not the profile of the Spokane serial killer.

Could the same person who killed Valiree, killed her mother, too? There was no doubt in my mind. It was simply a matter of finding physical evidence. Hide-n-seek— I was seeking to end the game.

Hours later, the Spokane County Sheriff's Detectives arrived at Sacred Heart Hospital and arrested Brad for second-degree murder. At the time, no motive had been established.

Brad already had a criminal record. It was for third-degree theft in 1991. He had stolen tires and wheels. Nothing else on record. At least, not yet.

After the dark shadows of winter and night shut down the day, authorities left the scene at Stevens County unsecured. A second body was not found— not yet.

❀ ❀ ❀

The Horror of It All

We left the gravesite when darkness came. It was such a long day for everyone. We were all exhausted. It was a difficult drive back.

It seemed like a very long hour in silence. While watching the headlights of cars and trucks pass by one by one, nothing much was said. The events of the day said it all. The horror of a little redheaded, 9-year-old girl was murdered.

I was shattered. How could something like this happen?

I went back to the hotel room in a daze. I wanted to wake up from this horrible nightmare. I knew that this was no dream. Valiree's death was for real and the reality knotted my guts with sickening rage.

I couldn't sleep, I just couldn't. I was hurting and I needed to talk to someone. I called my wife with the news and for consolation, but she couldn't help me, she was trying to cope with the devastating news herself.

I was so angry— so furious. Unable to sleep, I made many phone calls in the middle of the night. I guess it was a way for me to deal with all that anger, the grief, and pain that I was experiencing.

I called my dad, I called my brother in California, and I called Cynarra. I called friends. I called more family. I called people in town and people out of state.

We talked, we cried, we sobbed together. It was horrifying. What child deserves this? All I could see in my mind was Valiree, covered with dirt and all alone. It was so painful.

The pain I was experiencing was two fold, because I knew in my heart that Roseann was dead as well. The games that I had been playing with myself for the past seven years had to stop. I was forced to accept the reality that Roseann was gone and I could not bring her back. I will never be the same. In fact, life for me will never be the same. I learned a valuable lesson and that is life is too short— too precious to waste.

It hurts knowing that Valiree would never get the chance to go to the prom, to dance and laugh the night away with her high school friends. She will never get the chance to play soccer or cheerlead or learn to play the piano or guitar. She will never get the chance to drive a car or take skiing lessons and never get the chance to graduate from college, get a job, start a family, and have her own children.

Valiree just didn't get a chance to live a natural life and grow up to be a beautiful woman like her mother. All her chances were smothered; smothered because of a child killer.

I believe that Valiree and her mother are safe now. Nonetheless, there was still work that had to be done. Knowing that I couldn't help Roseann and Valiree anymore, I realized that others could be helped through their deaths.

Valiree was supposed to be going home that day to bake cookies with Grandma. She never made it to school. She never made it to her therapist.

With the news out about finding Valiree's body, I received many phone calls. I heard from people who suffered from the same sort of thing.

The community of Spokane doesn't deserve this. In fact, no community anywhere in this world deserves this.

❀ ❀ ❀

Was I Prepared?

I wasn't close to being prepared for the news when it finally came down the hill. I should have anticipated it, but how can a person control feeling a certain way about that which they do not what to accept?

From the time I got to the site that morning, to the time the grave was discovered, I was experiencing incredible anxiety, tension, and fear— all crowding for dominance within me. By the time I left, those feelings turned into intense pain. I had never experienced anything like that ever before.

It's not that I haven't experienced death in my family. It took a long time for me to accept my mother's death. She died in December of 1995. She was 58 years old.

She was admitted into Deaconess Hospital with walking pneumonia. Within 48 hours, she died of a heart attack. I had just spoken to her a few days earlier and she said she was fine. By the time I arrived from my home in Phoenix, she was lying on her deathbed.

When I went into her room, I quickly reached for her tender hand and held it between mine. My mom was unconscious.

She died that way and I don't know if she knew I was there— I never got to say good-bye. It happened so suddenly.

My previous trip to Spokane had been just three months earlier. My mom sat on her bed talking to me about Roseann and Valiree. She told me that she had a pain in her chest that just wouldn't go away.

My mother's physical pain was something she was accustomed to. The emotional pain she was experiencing had a lot to do with the stress that was caused when my sister mysteriously disappeared. For her last three years she had to live with not knowing what happened to her oldest daughter. My mom was in a lot of agony over that.

She wanted to believe that Roseann was in a Witness Protection Plan, but she knew better. Roseann had four kids. Who's going to put a mother in a Witness Protection Plan away from her kids? That doesn't happen and my mom knew that. She kept insisting that there would be no way Roseann would just walked away from her kids. There was no way in God's world that she would have done that.

Maybe it was a blessing for her not having the experience of finding out that her daughter and her granddaughter were murdered. I do not know how she would have handled that news. I do know however, that she would have been devastated just as I was.

No, I wasn't prepared. I could never be prepared to lose someone that was such an integral part of my life, someone I loved so dearly.

When Will the Tears Stop?

As the days went on, I played over in my mind the events leading up to Brad's arrest and the discovery of Valiree's body.

Valiree's murder investigation had widened to include her mother's disappearance. Brad was the last person to see Valiree and her mother alive. The sheriff was pooling information with the police. The FBI thought the link was strong enough for the two law enforcement agencies to share resources.

Although the Spokane Police were still in charge of my sister's investigation, Sheriff Sterk and his team were now helping to work on the case as well.

It was reported that the detectives felt that many of the witnesses in each case may very well have information regarding the other. They believed that Roseann's and Valiree's deaths might be connected.

In the meantime, I was working with my family to plan a memorial for Roseann. We finally accepted that Roseann was gone.

It was time to have a memorial service for her— it was time to let her go. I didn't want to go through with it, but this wasn't just about me.

We wanted Roseann's kids to have some kind of closure for their mom. It had been hard on them, not knowing if their mother was alive or not. Roseann's service would be after Valiree's and the public was invited to both.

I sat in my room that Wednesday night and recalled images of my sister and of Valiree when she was a baby. I sat and looked at their pictures.

Dear God, how I wished I could have saved Valiree.

Will the tears ever stop?

The GPS

When I watched the Channel 2 News on Wednesday night, November 17th, it was the first time that I had heard of the surveillance device known as the Global Positioning System (GPS). The Sheriff's department said they used the system to track Brad from what they thought was Valiree's first gravesite to the final one.

What was the GPS?

The way I understood it was that it was made up of three basic parts. Satellites, ground stations and user units. The satellites are the heart of the system, having 21 active satellites and 3 spare ones orbiting the earth above us. They use radio signals to locate exact distances from earth. Then they transmit these signals to the ground units on earth.

The main ground station that controls the satellites is located at Falcon Air Force Base in Colorado. However, there are other ground stations throughout the world. All of them track and monitor the satellites.

The user units are small devices that can be carried by hand or they can be placed on airplanes and vehicles. The tracking gear is packed in a small plastic box that was placed under Brad's truck. However, in order for the sheriff's department to know where Brad went in his truck, they had to get the small box back to read. The device was retrieved on Saturday night when Brad was found with a shotgun and taken to the hospital.

It is important to remember that the GPS device was included in the search warrants that were granted from Superior Court before Brad was arrested. Procedures were in order and followed with legal care.

The small user unit is about the size of a portable walkman or cell phone. The unit receives signals from three of the satellites orbiting the earth at any given time. The receiver estimates the distances from each of the satellites, giving a 3-D result. With a few math calculations, the location is known. The sheriff's department used a GPS, the tracking unit, to determine where Brad's truck had been driven.

Using a GPS device for tracking suspects is like having a private detective tracking someone and finding where they had been. In criminal cases, I think the GPS is much safer to use and should be encouraged. An innocent person like a detective would never be in danger by trying to follow someone who is suspected of criminal behavior if the GPS unit is available instead.

Jackson's attorney was stating that the use of the GPS was against Brad's Constitutional rights.

Oh no, Brad can't possibly get off. He just can't! A killer can't possibly have a constitutional right to be freed on a technicality. There's so much physical evidence against him and he still might get off? That's utterly ridiculous to even think that any technicality can free a murderer. Great, let's get a killer back into society!

I don't think that is what the Founding Fathers of the U.S. Constitution had in mind for future generations. So how can our present legal system imply that someone who commits one of the worst crime has a chance to be set free?

Land of the free? It's not free for murderers and we're not free to free murderers. It can't be freedom for anyone who commits a heinous crime.

Well, I know that Brad's defense will try all kinds of tricks to get him off. Trying to use a technicality or crying, "a violation of Constitutional rights" would be a poor excuse for releasing any child-murderer back into the world. It can't happen. As caretakers of our children, we should not let murderers be free.

The Ghoulish Job

After I had heard the evidence against Brad I tried to envision what could have happen to provoke him to do this. I wondered if Valiree did something that angered him. I tried to picture him murdering her, but could not imagine that. What was wrong with him to do this?

I kept watching the images in my mind, captivated and motionless as if I was in a stupor. I imagined what happened when Brad was close to being exposed. He wanted to keep his crime hidden. This is what I imagine he did.

His vehicle moved slowly into the shadows of the night. The headlights were turned off. He knew the road and the place where he wanted to park.

He pulled up to the spot and turned the ignition off. Sitting in the driver's seat, he waited to see if he was being followed or if anyone was close by. He listened carefully for any sound of movement.

Nervously, he looked around and waited. His clothes were soaked with sweat as he methodically thought through the steps that he needed to take.

He reached for the handle and quietly opened the door, then slid out of his truck.

He slyly removed his back brace. It was pre-scribed for a back injury caused on a water slide in August with his daughter. He slipped the brace in a plastic bag to keep it clean and set it down on the seat. He then grabbed the shovel next to him.

Carefully walking to the site, he spotted where he had buried her. He removed the pine boughs that covered the mound of dirt. He cursed the ground because it hadn't frozen yet. The snow hadn't fallen either and here it was mid-November. He was expect-ing ice, snow, and colder weather by now. Mother Nature's clock was off.

He poked the shovel around feeling for loose ground. Locating the right spot, he didn't have to dig too deep. He should have buried her deeper, but he didn't have much time back then.

All he needed was to get one end dug up where the feet were, then pull the body out. He quickly detected it.

He grabbed the ankles, tugging and pulling hard. It was dead weight, hindered by the ground around it.

He didn't want to dig too much, so he pulled harder. Hard enough that he lost his balance and fell backwards. The plastic bags that he had wrapped around her head came off along with the duct tape that didn't stick.

Wildly he looked around, listening with his burning ears. His heart was thumping loud and sweat trickled down his body.

Finally, he freed the corpse from its grave!

Not wanting to waste any more time there, he struggled to pick up the decaying body.

own flesh and blood— a daughter that he loved.

Assuring himself that she had asked for it, he kicked the body into a plastic bag. After dragging it to the vehicle, he threw it carelessly onto the floor.

He was breathing hard and felt hot. He tried brushing off the dirt, but it stuck to him. He'll have to take care of that later.

He mustn't miss anything— get the ground smoothed out, stomp it down, cover it again with the boughs, and get out of there. Get that body back in the ground. Fast— do it fast, so no one will ever find it.

Sitting behind the steering wheel, he could feel her brown eyes staring through the dirty plastic bag. She was peering at him. The skin from her mouth was rotting and pulling away. She looked like she was smiling at him, a deadly grin, as if she enjoyed the desperate predicament he was in. A shiver of fear crept up his spine.

The odor was bad. He had to roll down the window for fresh air. It never occurred to him that he was the one who stank more.

He was angry, seeing red again, leaving Dishman-Mica in an evil rage. They were only five miles from home, he had to go farther.

As much as he hated it, they had to make another trip together and it was all someone else's fault.

He drove to Hunter's Road in Stevens County, one of his familiar hunting spots. It was near Springdale, roughly 60 miles away.

He scowled at the decaying body. She had been haunting him like hell for almost four weeks.

Soon, she would hold him accountable.

It was difficult getting the job done with the darkness around him. He couldn't control that. In haste, he dug a shallow grave. It was too dark to do a thorough job. He had more to do and daylight would provide him a better chance.

Then it was morning, Saturday, November 13th. After cleaning up and planning his next move, he drove out to a long-time female friend in his 1985 Honda Accord. This was one of his decoys. He visited with her for a few hours, then drove a couple blocks over to Decatur. This was where he once lived with Roseann in 1992. His neighbor and friend still lived next to his old house.

The neighbor loaned Brad his 1979 Ford truck. He left his Honda at his friend's house and headed back out to find Valiree's corpse.

It was a long drive, but it gave him time to think about his planned performance. He reviewed in his head what he had to do next.

He had already dug up and reburied the body. However, it had been very dark that night and he knew the grave was too shallow. He would move it again, farther into the wooded area. Far enough where no one would find the body.

He knew the area well. It was a favorite place to hunt— he'd been there many times before. As he turned off the main road, he began wondering when the bad weather would come. The weather was bound to change soon. Ice storm '97 came around this time. So where was the ice and snow that he was depending on? He knew his timing wasn't off. It just wasn't a normal season.

As he was cursing the mild weather that complicated his life, he turned onto Hunters Road. He thought he spotted the place.

He pulled off to the side and got out. He looked around, but couldn't find anything. His eyes darted maniacally back and forth across the ground—nothing. That wasn't the right place! He looked around more, but was having a hard time. He couldn't have forgotten where it was. He was just there last night!

He got back into the truck driving slowly, further down the road. He thought he recognized the spot and stopped the truck again. He stepped out to investigate more closely. He thought he heard something and glanced up the road. He noticed a hunter and his kid watching him intently, obviously wondering what he was doing. He cursed and hoped they hadn't recognized him. He couldn't get to the site without being seen. He would have to wait.

Things didn't look good. He was so close, yet so far from being done— a mile and an eternity. He had to leave without causing any suspicion.

Casually returning to the truck, he drove away. Having to drive another 60 miles back to Decatur allowed him time to smolder with rage. He knew who was responsible for all this.

He'd have to ruin another day by searching for the site, digging up the body and moving it again. He was tired of all this mess.

Irritated and preoccupied, he quickly returned the Ford pickup to his friends. Few words exchanged and he left the friends wondering about his anxiety. He left his shovel in their truck with no mention.

98

Running back to his car, he cautiously drove to the Fairfield Inn and parked his car. He didn't want to attract any attention. He placed a shotgun on the back seat directly behind him. Anxieties led to hostilities. Hostilities rekindled hate. Someone needed to pay for this and he knew exactly who.

Assault, Money, and Prayer

"John, we have something to tell you. Valiree's body has been cremated."

"Cremated? Cremated? How can we view her body when it's been cremated?"

I became very upset. I wanted to see Valiree one last time. All I had left were her pictures, now she was gone— gone forever.

Why did this happen? Why did the cremation take place so fast? Who made that decision? I wanted to know.

"Because of her deformed and decayed body, it appeared to be the right and only thing to do," said the funeral director.

I had no choice. I had to accept the speedy cremation, at least until I got the full autopsy report.

Now for sure, there is no more pain for dear sweet Valiree. No more. She can't be hurt anymore. I thanked God for that.

Tuesday, after the discovery of Valiree's body, Brad was arraigned. I watched Brad's arraignment at the courthouse around 2:00. It could only be viewed by closed-circuit television.

Brad was the first one up. Murder charges were filed against him. The autopsy found that Valiree died of homicidal violence. He appeared to show no emotion as he pleaded "not guilty."

Well, I guess that was one way to say it. Is there anything else to be added to the charge? Can we add assault? What about transporting a dead body from grave to grave to hide the evidence? Was second-degree murder the best that could be done?

Prosecutors argued that Jackson posed a serious risk to the community in part because of falsely reporting that Valiree was missing four weeks ago.

How many other parts were there? One part was good enough to set bail, I suppose, but there are other missing parts. I sure hope they will be adding them soon.

Brad's bail was set at only $1 million and that infuriated me. I didn't think that he should have been released, bail or not— for anyone, especially when the evidence against him was so overwhelming and exact.

If someone Brad knows could come up with a million in cash or property, he could walk. That's just infuriating!

Here's the system— act like you're innocent until proven guilty. Even if there's undeniable cold, hard evidence against you; walk in with evidence— walk out with bail. Too good for the guilty and too bad for us.

It's not fair. It's not right for those of us who live within the law. It's not fair to the victim. I'll say it again— it's not and will never be fair to us.

Here's a person who's accused of one of the worst crimes known to humanity and he could be set free. Any person whose been accused of doing what Brad is accused of doing, has no business being on any street. If human life is not respected, especially a child's life, then the severest punishment the law will allow should be given. If a person is guilty of murdering their own child, then that severest punishment should be expedited.

The medical examiner ruled out gunshot or stab wounds as a cause of death— but called Valiree's death a result of "homicidal violence."

I wondered what "homicidal violence" meant? Did it mean that Valiree was beaten to death?

The motive remains a mystery, but detectives were pursuing evidence of sexual abuse. Bloodstains were found on Valiree's pillow, two of Brad's pubic hairs were found on her bed sheets, hairs were retrieved from Valiree's grave. This just angered me because she was so innocent.

In the state of Washington, the second-degree murder charge could bring as little as five years. Yes, only five years! I have a real hard time with that. Somehow that punishment doesn't seem to fit the crime. It makes me feel like a victim myself. That's outrageous!

The sheriff's chaplain, Keith Kirkingburg called to inform me of the time and date of Valiree's funeral. It would be on Saturday, November 20th, at 11:00am. It would be held at Valiree's school, McDonald Elementary.

The chaplain helped to set up the arrangements and the program. My dad would do the opening prayer and I would do the closing prayer. Valiree's brother Joktan would sing at both funerals. The first funeral was for Valiree.

"By the way, John, I just heard that Brad wants to be there."

I was shocked.

How could he possibly be at Valiree's funeral? Wasn't he in jail?

Later I found out that in certain situations, a prisoner can be allowed to attend a family member's funeral.

"Now John, could you make sure nothing is said or done if he shows up? This is a day for Valiree so we don't want to ruin it for her."

I agreed, and then hung up.

My God, if Brad was going to be there, that's something that will be hard to swallow. I can handle it, but I will have to concentrate on everything for Valiree and totally forget about him. How could he come to Valiree's funeral? Brad Jackson is the accused killer. He's the one accused of ending Valiree's life. The evidence shows that he buried her once, then dug up her body, and reburied it again.

I was not about to let the accused bury Valiree a third time.

I thought about the children at Valiree's school. I thought about the teachers and the parents.

What kind of message would this send to them?

When I found out he could be allowed to attend the funeral, my first approach to preventing this was to go to the radio and television stations.

I was going to try to prevent him from coming. I would take it to the streets.

I went to the TV reporters and told them of my fears. I did stories with all of them. This was my way of fighting. I told them the truth. What Brad was accused of doing, there was no way I could let him show up in front of the kids at the funeral.

"Let's just go out and round up all the killers out there. Why not let Charles Manson out, if this is how it works? Let the kids wonder what the heck is going on in our society. Great lesson in civics, right? We cannot let Brad Jackson out to attend the funeral of the victim he's accused of killing."

Thank God every station played the story.

"We cannot let Brad Jackson out."

While I was running all over town telling everyone that we couldn't allow an accused killer to come to the victims funeral, I stopped by KXLY TV and Radio, the ABC local affiliate.

Mark Fuhrman, the Los Angeles Policeman who worked on the O.J. Simpson case, was working in Spokane. He, along with Mike Fitzsimmons, hosted a radio show every Thursday on KXLY 920 AM.

When I stopped by to see Brian Paul, the marketing director for KXLY, he took me upstairs to meet Mark and Mike. They, along with their manager, Jim Bickel, and producer April Scott, were very sympathetic toward my situation. They asked me if I would like to participate with them on their talk show. I accepted.

As we were taking calls from listeners, a news flash from KXLY Television came across the airway.

Trova Hutchins, their reporter, reported that the charges against Brad Jackson had been moved up from second-degree murder to first-degree murder.

That was good news!

It was now murder one and Brad, if convicted, could possibly face the death penalty.

Now I know he won't be coming to Valiree's funeral.

❀ ❀ ❀

A Mother's Love

After the radio broadcast, I returned to my room at the Quality Inn and found many messages waiting for me. People were calling to tell me about their experiences with Valiree.

One of my callers told me about one of Valiree's science projects in school. It had to do with Alka Seltzer. The experiment didn't turn out the same way for everyone. Since time was running out and Valiree wasn't quite done, the teacher gave her some extra "plop-n-fizz" tablets to take home to have her mother help her finish the project.

"I don't have a mommy. My mommy left me."

That's what Valiree said. That's what Valiree thought her mommy did—leave her. How sad and unfortunate that Valiree didn't get a chance to know her mother and know that her mother loved her.

"Listen, Valiree, it doesn't mean that your mom doesn't love you. It doesn't mean that she didn't care.

Things happen and maybe she wasn't ready to be a mommy, but it doesn't mean that your mommy didn't love you. I'm sure when you were in your mommy's stomach, she loved you very much. She loves you now Valiree, wherever she is. Your mommy loves you very much and she always will."

I take great comfort in knowing that that teacher was a caring and loving person, as many teachers are.

❀ ❀ ❀

Midnight Realities

I had the worst thought ever. What I was going through was really happening— this nightmare was really happening! To kill a child and actually do what Brad Jackson is accused of doing gave me great difficulty. How could a father do that? How?

I wanted to find Valiree alive— not dead, especially not the way she was found.

I was aghast. How could I let this happen? I asked myself as if I was actually guilty for her death. It was as if I was holding myself responsible for not finding her in time.

I jumped up out of bed and ran into the bathroom. I looked in the mirror searching for reality. What was happening to me? What?

As I was looking in the mirror my expressions changed. I felt like I was dreaming, but I was awake. It was like being chased by someone and not being able to get away from them.

Then I began to understand. The pieces to the mystery I had been living with started to make sense. The dreams I was having about my sister had come true. Valiree had been in trouble and through my dreams, I had been getting the messages. They had been telling me of things to come. I had no idea that I would be thrust into them. With very little sleep, the night passed, and the morning was upon me.

❀ ❀ ❀

A Full Day Ahead

Why did I call for a funeral? Was I going to be able to handle it?

I was trying to find enough strength to go on. It was going to be hard and I wasn't sure if I wanted closure yet.

I understand that people die— that's just the way it is. Why must it be a child— and why this way? A precious life smothered away. I was having a hard time dealing with Valiree's death and the way she died.

I thought about my mom. When my mom died in 1995, she told me to continue to search for Roseann and not to forget about Valiree.

She was very distressed and I assured her that I would continue to search for Roseann and try to find where Valiree was.

I know that my mom would have had trouble with her granddaughter's murder. It could have killed her— killed her of a broken heart. It was hard to think about.

I started the morning with a phone call to the County Sheriff's Department. I invited everyone there to come to the funerals. I called the television and radio stations and invited them, too. I left word that the funerals were open to the public and the entire community was invited. Anybody and everybody could attend and say what they wanted to, in memorial to Valiree and her mother.

Valiree's funeral was moved from her school to a church. Brad would not attend, especially after he was charged with first-degree murder. I didn't think the community would have welcomed him anyway.

The services would be at eleven in the morning for Valiree and three o'clock in the afternoon for Roseann. Brad's mother wanted a short service and wanted to show a video of Valiree.

I was just about to leave my room for the day to make sure that everything was ready for the funerals— then my phone rang.

I picked it up and heard the voice of a woman. She said that she had information about Brad. She had known him for the past 11 or 12 years and had known Roseann as well. She knew about the problems that Roseann and Brad had had seven years ago and she wanted to talk to me.

Well, if that was the case, I wanted to talk to her too. I took her address and told her that I would see her after I took care of the final plans for the funerals the next day. I would meet her later that afternoon.

I had a full day ahead of me with planning the funeral and a curiously interesting planned visit with the mysterious caller.

❃ ❃ ❃

None of That

Before I left to see the mystery woman, I left information of my whereabouts at the front desk of the hotel where I was staying, the Quality Inn. I also left the address with Steve, telling him that I would check in with them when I got back. I didn't know what to expect.

It was around 4:30 when I pulled out of the hotel parking lot. It was already dark. It took about an hour to get there. When I arrived, I was greeted at the door and asked to come in.

The woman immediately made it very clear that she did not want to get involved. She was emphatic about it, which is why I can not use her name.

She used to live next door to Brad when Roseann lived with him. She remembered Brad dating a girl named Becky, but she hadn't seen Becky since they broke up.

I didn't see the connection of what she was telling me at first. There were a lot of details that needed to be explained, but I didn't want to slow her down with questions— so I let her talk.

She told me that she would have never suspected that Brad could kill his daughter.

"Whenever Brad and Valiree would visit, she would sit next to him saying the same thing over and over again, "I love you, Daddy. I love you, Daddy," looking up at him for approval. Looking back, it was so unusual the way Valiree would sit and say the words, I love you, Daddy. It seemed so unnatural."

She mentioned how Brad had come by her house a week after Valiree was missing. He was angry with his mom because all she did was cry about her Valiree.

"My Valiree, my Valiree, my Valiree."

"It was not her Valiree," he exclaimed, it was his baby, not hers.

During the summer, Brad supposedly hurt his back at the water park with Valiree and because of this, he was still living in his parents' home. He was advised by his doctors to wear a back brace and since then, was not working.

Brad told her that his present girlfriend kicked him out of her house because he wouldn't marry her. They lived together for more than two years with her two children and Valiree. Valiree and his girlfriend did not get along.

I got the girlfriend's name, hoping I could talk to her, too.

The woman told me how guilty she felt after Valiree's body was found. She had been a close friend to Brad and had been praying for him.

She felt cheated and betrayed by his deception. She thought she could have saved Valiree's life. She felt responsible for Valiree's and— Roseann's death as well.

I didn't quite follow her logic, but I determined that she genuinely was feeling a lot of guilt. I wasn't sure why she felt responsible for Valiree's and her mother's deaths, but I didn't blame her, I couldn't, I was just grateful that she was talking to me.

She told me how Brad used to dance for extra money.

"It was between 1993 and 1994, that he used to strip down for parties."

On Saturday, October 23rd, she and Brad were standing outside in front of her house. Brad received a call on his cell-phone from his sister Debbie. He was immediately agitated.

" I'd never seen him like this before. He was asking Debbie if they had found Valiree. The sheriff detectives had taped off his property that day and had come back for another search. For some reason, Brad hung up on her, grabbed my cell-phone, and called her right back. He began pacing back and forth with a worried look on his face and worried sound in his voice. After a few minutes, he handed the phone back to me and said that he had to get home.

The next day I drove out to Brad's house to pick-up more fliers. My girlfriend and I had already gone through all the fliers that he had given us. He met me at the front door, took me through the house, showed me Valiree's room, and we went back out front.

Brad knew what all his neighbors were doing the day Valiree disappeared. He told me that the old lady across the street usually sits by her piano in her front room. She always waved to Valiree. That morning she was on her back porch feeding the squirrels. The man next door worked graveyard. Usually, he's coming home when Brad walked Valiree to school. However, on that particular morning, he was working another shift or something. It was strange to me that Brad knew what his neighbors were doing."

On another occasion, Saturday, November 13th, the day after Valiree's body was moved, Brad stopped by her house. He mentioned that he and I had spoken and that he would see to it that I would never see Valiree again. He had her thinking that I was trying to become a movie star or something and that was why I was in town.

He went to her computer and pulled up a picture of Valiree. She said, "Valiree's photo was placed on some website and Brad knew where to go to find it. He touched her picture gently on the screen and cried, that's my baby. I want to find my baby."

He was crying and she felt so sorry for him. She wanted to help him so she comforted him as any compassionate friend would do.

Then she walked with him out to his car. Although they had never been romantically involved, Brad attempted to change that.

"Brad pulled me forcibly next to him thrusting his groin against me, but I pushed him back, scolding him. I asked, how could you even think about that now? I'll have none of that! None of it! I turned away and walked back into my house."

After I had been there an hour or so, her phone rang. It was Steve— he was concerned.

111

I had been there for two hours and it was time to go. It had been a long day and I was very tired. I had heard enough.

I ended my visit with the understanding that besides me, the mystery woman would only talk to the police.

❈ ❈ ❈

The Funerals

What a short time we have on this planet.

At 10:00am, Steve, Jodel and their daughter picked me up from the hotel. We drove over to the Valley Fourth Memorial Church in the Spokane Valley. They dropped me off in front of the church before parking the car.

Many people greeted me at the door. People I hadn't seen in years. There was Maria Poydras— our families had grown up together. Alice Moore— her son Michael and I were best friends during our school years. There were church members from Calvary Baptist— they were there as friends.

I shook hands and hugged many including the chaplain, Kirkingburg, Sheriff Sterk and his wife. My friend and pastor of Calvary Baptist Church, Reverend C.W. Andrews was there for support as he and his family had always been.

As I entered before the service, I looked toward the front of the sanctuary. The pews were filled. My eyes caught the framed photograph of Valiree and I was immediately overcome with grief.

Instead of going to my seat, I went downstairs away from the crowd. I had to get away to compose myself. I cried and cried while trying to hide.

All I could think about was Valiree, our redheaded angel. Finally, I forced myself back upstairs before the service began.

I felt as if I was in a trance. My movement was without volition. It was an eerie state of existence that I couldn't control. It got worse as Reverend Andrews, Chaplain Kirkinburg, and I made our way down the aisle to the pulpit.

Listening to all the crying, wailing and sniffling was so sad— so very sad.

Then I looked up through my tears and saw Valiree's picture again. Her gentle and warm smile only intensified my grief.

On the lit wooden altar were etched the words, "In Remembrance of Me," which held the picture of Valiree. Placed next to the words was a drawing of her and her cousin playing ball. A white teddy bear leaned against her picture with a bouquet of flowers on each side. A large heart-shaped wreath of colorful flowers with an angel stood next to the pile of stuffed animals that were laid below her picture. Karen, Valiree's grandmother, was the one responsible for the tribute to her. I was grateful for her touch. Two arrangements of pink and purple balloons hung nearby. They were colors that Valiree was wearing when she was found.

There were four seats, but only three speakers. The fourth seat, I guessed, was for my dad. My dad was scheduled to give the opening prayer, but he was too upset to attend. He asked his pastor and friend Reverend Andrews to give the prayer in his place.

Chaplain Kirkinburg and Pastor Andrews took the two seats on the far right with the chaplain in the middle. I took the seat on the left.

There was a space between the chaplain and me which was intentional on my part, because I wanted to be close to Valiree's picture. I wanted to be as close to her as possible.

The service began with the opening prayer from Pastor Andrews. Next was the Spokane Area Children's Chorus. They sang Valiree's favorite song, "You Are My Sunshine." Later they sang, "Jesus Loves Me." Such simple songs with so much meaning. My tears kept flowing as they sang. In fact, I cried throughout the entire service. I found myself overwhelmed with emotion, then the video was shown.

When the video started, the first picture was of Roseann holding Valiree. Then came pictures of Valiree showing different stages of her life; what she did and what she liked. The video ended with her last birthday, October 6, 1999. The video was informative, heart-felt, and warm— a real tearjerker.

Joktan, Valiree's brother appeared next on the program. He sang his version of, "Tears in Heaven," a song written by Eric Clapton after he lost his son. When Joktan finished, I was still crying.

I went to Spokane to find Valiree and her mother alive and ended attending their funerals— this caused me great pain.

"I cannot do two things you want me to. I can't take away your pain and I can't bring Valiree back."

This was how the chaplain began his eulogy with a white handkerchief in his hand. His voice cracked. I could tell, it was hard on him too.

"Not one of us wanted things to turn out this way, but after we weep, beloved joy will come in the morning."

Some of the joys in Valiree's life were mentioned. She liked making Jell-O, dressing up like a cowgirl, playing Frisbee, and trying to fish but squirming about the worms.

"It's not the length of life, but the depth. Valiree plowed deeply. In those nearly 4,000 days God graced us with Valiree, she left her indelible mark upon us."

As the chaplain was finishing the eulogy, I realized that soon it would be my turn. I was supposed to close with the Lord's Prayer as printed on the program.

As I stood at the podium my tears continued to flow. Chaplain Kirkinburg stood behind me to keep me steady. I was relieved that the Lord's Prayer was printed on the programs because I needed everyone's help to read it.

When the service ended, the hugs and handshakes continued. Pastor Andrews could be seen praying with people who needed prayer.

The local television news crews were all represented. On the way to the car, I stopped and gave a comment about the community support and turnout.

Our family and friends went back to the Quality Inn and rested in preparation for the three o' clock service.

❀ ❀ ❀

The Rest of the Day

When it was time, we drove to the Redeemer Lutheran Church for the service. Sandy Anderson, one of the Elders of the church, had been gracious to invite our family to have the service at his church. They are a wonderful group of people.

Seven years and no word from my sister. When Valiree's body was found, I knew Roseann was dead, but I still didn't want to accept it. However, her children needed closure. They love their mom and believe that she will always be with them.

The service began with my dad's opening prayer. He had mustered up enough strength this time. Bless his heart. He had some humble and warm words to say. It wasn't the words that I remembered as much as it was the tone in his voice, it was one of love and grief. When I heard the names of Roseann and Valiree flow from his lips, I started crying again. Then I realized that this was painful for the rest of the family as well.

Roseann's oldest daughter, Cynarra, read the Psalm 23, you know— "The Lord is my Shepherd, I shall not want."

Then we sang "Amazing Grace." Sandy read Bible verses from Chapter 5 of Corinthians.

After the scriptures were read, children and adults read their poems that they had written for Roseann and Valiree. They were beautiful. One of Valiree's teachers read a poem crying the entire time. Everyone seemed touched.

Teachers and other staff members seemed so devastated by all of this. I appreciated their support.

We all chuckled while recalling Roseann's cooking. Her Thanksgiving dinners were a specialty that will be remembered along with her blooper pancakes and bad oatmeal. Laughter and tears accompanied the memories.

The message of Roseann and Valiree, mother and child, was one of love and of tragedy. Both were kind, sweet, and giving. Their lives were short, but were filled with love. We will have to take comfort in believing that they are united again in heaven.

Joktan, ended the service by singing again "Tears in Heaven." However this time he sang without the accompaniment of music. His voice was beautiful, just as it was earlier with music.

A son was singing for his mother.

Touched by the sadness of it all, we left hand-in-hand, arm-in-arm, heart to-heart, to the nearby gymnasium. Prepared snacks and sandwiches were set up for us to enjoy.

The Spokane community of caring people helped release much of the pressure that had built up inside of me during the previous weeks. The pain in my face was gone. It felt like a healing was taking place.

A news reporter asked me if it was over.

"No, it's not over. We will continue to look for Roseann's body. We will not stop until it's found."

Afterwards, we went to dinner, compliments of Longhorn Barbecue, in the banquet room of the Quality Inn. The Quality Inn's GM and Sales Director had set up the room for our family. Quality individuals at the Quality Inn, that's exactly what I found.

I returned to my room around 9:30 after everyone had left for the night. It was a long day, but an important one. I needed sleep, but I was still restless and disturbed.

Before going to bed, I picked up an envelope given to me at the first funeral. The children at McDonald Elementary had written poems for Valiree. One of Valiree's teachers gave me the envelope after the funeral.

It was after 11:00 when I finally fell asleep while reading their words of comfort.

❀ ❀ ❀

Valiree's Church

"Mr. Stone, we would love to have you come to our church today. Just come by and say hello, to make your presence known. It would be a help to all of us. Please come by."

I received an invitation to visit Valiree's church in Deer Park. Valiree and Brad both were members. Several members invited me that Sunday morning the day after Valiree's funeral. I really didn't feel like going. Nonetheless, they were part of Valiree's family, too.

As I was leaving the hotel, Roseann's other children were in the lobby. They were getting ready with Don, their father, to go back to Kennewick. Don had made the trip with other family members to say goodbye to Roseann and Valiree. He had to go back home and go to work. Angelica, Roseann's middle daughter, had school on Monday.

We said our good-byes and I left to meet my brother, James and his wife, Janice. They had arrived right before Roseann and Valiree's funeral. I was happy to see them and appreciated that they were there with me.

When I arrived at the Courtyard Inn, where they were staying, we decided to take their car to Valiree's church. As we pulled away from the parking lot, it started snowing. The snow wasn't fine or powdery— but large flakes that poured profusely.

Being from California, my brother wasn't use to driving in that kind of weather. We slipped and slid all over the road. It was scary, but thrilling as well.

Fortunately, we made it to the church. Sonja Johnson, the pastor, greeted me with a long hug. Her sincerity and grief were strong— I could feel her sorrow.

I had several stops to make that day, so I spoke at the beginning of the service. Standing before the congregation, I read some of the poems that the children from school had written about Valiree. They were the same words that gave me comfort the night before. After sharing the beautiful verses, I commented,

"Brad Jackson is a child of God!"

There was silence. I guess they couldn't believe their ears. I knew that Brad had volunteered to help this church make their handicap rail a few months ago and everyone knew how I felt about Brad.

"Yes, Brad Jackson is a child of God and God will deal with him. I don't have hatred toward him, but yes, I have a lot of anger. I don't have hatred because he is still God's child."

I started thinking of Valiree again.

"Valiree is an angel. Valiree would want no one to feel guilty."

It was hard to hold back. I was trying to control my tears, I felt the heartache swell up inside me again.

"I just want everyone to know in this church that Valiree loves all of you."

I couldn't say anymore. The tears were coming fast. It was time to leave.

As I was going out the door, a woman standing in the back stopped me. She was shaking, really shaking with emotion.

"Oh, about what you said about Brad being a child of God and about Valiree being with the Lord and she's an angel. Oh, I just felt compelled to tell you who l am."

She handed me a piece of paper with her name and phone number on it. I looked at the name and couldn't believe my eyes. It was Brad's girlfriend— his current one!

She stood there crying like a beautiful flower weeping raindrops. I jotted down my number for her and hoped that we could talk. I prayed to God that we could talk soon.

Searching on a Snowy Sunday

After leaving Valiree's church— James, Janice, and I had planned to go out where Valiree's body was found. Detectives were scouring the area for another grave near Valiree's.

The FBI behavioral experts advised the local detectives to look closer at the site and closer at Brad. The police department was investigating Brad's whereabouts at the time of Roseann's disappearance.

"Somebody out there knows something. Maybe we'll get a break like we did in Valiree's case."

Could Brad's girlfriend be that break?

It was snowing hard and we couldn't see the ground anymore. Since it was getting more slippery and we didn't have snow tires, we headed back to town. Besides, I couldn't wait to get in touch with Brad's girlfriend.

❁ ❁ ❁

Sunday Night Phone Calls

I had several different phone calls Sunday night, but the one I was interested in the most was the one from Brad's girlfriend. I called her back that night and it seemed as though our conversation lasted for hours.

She and Brad had been together since early 1997. They lived together in Deer Park with Valiree and her two children, who were 8 and 12 years old, until February of 1999.

She told me that she couldn't get through to Valiree. Valiree had, as she explained it, an attachment disorder.

"She trusted no one. She was a very unhappy child. The smiles were good when the camera came out, but it was just a face, a painted face. Valiree was not happy; she pouted a lot."

According to the girlfriend, Valiree's depression continued to worsen. Brad and Valiree started going to church in 1997 on Easter. They were members for two years and were baptized April 3, 1999.

Valiree did not get along with Brad's girlfriend. Brad had to move out of her house, but the girlfriend still loved him.

"I was ready to get married, but Brad kept putting me off. He felt he was doing fine just the way he was. Except he did have to get Valiree help because Valiree and I were having problems getting along."

Brad's girlfriend talked a lot about Brad and Valiree. Valiree's favorite color was red, not purple like everyone was thinking, and that Valiree liked Dalmatians and little kittens.

"Oh by the way, Brad has been calling me from jail. He just wanted to let me know that he doesn't remember doing any of the stuff that he was being accused of."

I asked her if she believed what he said. She paused choosing her words carefully.

"Brad is very deceptive, by no means is he insane."

My conversation with Brad's girlfriend left me more confused than ever. I wondered what Valiree's life was like before she attended McDonald Elementary— before she was put on Paxil, an antidepressant. What was the cause of all this? Certainly there were reasons, there had to be.

The Brick Wall

After my conversation with Brad's girlfriend I returned another telephone call.

The mystery woman that I had previously talked to, called to inform me of a suspicion that she had regarding the basement in Brad's old house.

"Around the time your sister disappeared, Brad had been doing some brick and or cement work in the basement of his home. I remember the time well because it was during a vacation that my parents took to Disney. I lived right down the street from Brad so I was over there a lot. Valiree was always running around the house sliding in her socks, she was so small then. What I found to be real strange back then was the dog that Brad got.

The dog was either a Siberian Husky or something similar. The dog was so vicious. I remember thinking about the dog being around tiny Valiree. It was as if the dog just appeared one day. The dog wouldn't let anyone near the house without Brad being close. For that period of time, it seemed as though Brad was always in his basement. John, do you think Roseann could be buried down there? "
I told her that I would be out to her house first thing in the morning.

Chills were going up and down my body. I was deeply saddened. That night was filled with terror. Only months ago I had watched a movie where a teen- age girl was buried behind a brick wall in a basement. I cried and cried. All I could see was Roseann behind a brick wall.

If she is behind a wall or under cement, was she alive at first? Was my sister buried alive? Did she call out for me? Winnie, Winnie help me?

I couldn't sleep. I was scared of what I might see. I came so close to going out to Brad's old house that night. When the morning came, I showered, got dressed and headed out to the home of the mystery woman.

When I arrived she let me in and we sat on the couch. We started our conversation again about Brad's basement. After a few minutes, I told her that I needed her to talk to the police. She became so angry.

"The police didn't question me or my friends seven years ago. In fact, from my understanding, no one in the neighborhood knew Roseann mysteriously disappeared. Here we were Brad's friends and neighbors and yet the police didn't question us. John, you must be so upset with the police. Valiree could possibly still be alive if they would have done their job seven years ago. They devalued your sister and left Valiree unprotected. Now you want me to talk to the police. John, Brad refused the lie-detector test back then, why didn't they do more?"

Her comments shocked me. She told me that she would talk to the police only if I was present. I used her phone and called a detective.

The detective showed up with his partner around 3:00 that day. They were invited in and the fireworks began.

They both sat down on the couch while the woman and I sat on her loveseat. One of the detectives pulled out a notepad and began asking her questions. She told them all the things she told me over the past few days. Except for one of the detectives, the rest of us sat there drinking coffee. We must have drunk a couple of pots.

Speaking to the detectives, I said that I knew they had families and that I knew that neither one of them wanted Valiree or Roseann to lose their lives. They both looked so sad. I actually felt sorry for them.

Then all at once, the woman started asking questions. She asked them why in the world didn't they look her up before now?

"If you guys would have done a better job investigating Roseann's disappearance seven years ago, Valiree might be alive today." Angrily she asked them how they slept at night?

After she finished questioning them, they told her that another detective would be getting in touch with her. The detectives and I left her home and stood out front and continued our talk.

They asked, "What are you going to do about checking out Brad's old house?"

I said that I wanted to check it out and that I would give them a few hours to get a search warrant.

While waiting to get the warrant, I became anxious and decided to go on without it and investigate Brad's old house on my own.

I picked up my uncle, Mike. I knew that we couldn't trespass on the property without authorization from the residents. I knocked and the resident allowed us to go in.

I went directly into the basement. Mike, the occupant, and I together inspected the walls and floor. We were in the dark. None of us knew anything about concrete. The occupant told us that we could come back with dogs and search again if we liked. Disappointedly we left. I decided that after Thanksgiving I would go back and search the house again.

Meanwhile, Brad's arraignment for first-degree murder was delayed. I had to leave just to get my head together, to put my emotions aside, and to proceed with what needed to be done next. The distance between Phoenix and Spokane would be good for awhile.

✿ ✿ ✿

Thanksgiving

Thanksgiving holiday was upon me. I wanted to be home with my wife and children, and they wanted me home, too. I had been gone since November 9th and it had been a rough two weeks.

The time away from Spokane would give me time to write letters thanking people for what they had done during the whole ordeal concerning Valiree. I planned to return after Thanksgiving. I had much to be thankful for. I had much more to do.

I went back home to Arizona Wednesday morning November 24th, staying for the rest of the week.

❀ ❀ ❀

Stacking Up the Evidence

Thanksgiving came and went. It was as though I never left Spokane. There was unfinished business left to complete. Now that I believed without a doubt, that Roseann was dead, I would try and find her body. I didn't think to look for her body seven years ago and gave up searching for her.
I wasn't about to give up now.

Although Valiree was found, there was still a lot of unfinished business. I felt as though I should continue to represent Valiree, as her mom would have. Since her mother was not here, I felt I should be her representative.

Before we knew it, my wife was driving me back to the airport again. We said our good-byes and I hopped back on Southwest Airlines.

I arrived back in Spokane on Monday, November 29th. Again, Steve picked me up from the airport. He drove me to the Fairfield Inn. I was there for the following two weeks.

Court documents were released on Wednesday suggesting a possible motive for Valiree's murder. The Affidavit of Probable Cause stated that Brad Jackson "repeatedly and inappropriately violated" the personal boundaries of his daughter in the months leading up to her murder. In her diary, Valiree wrote that her father embarrassed her in front of her friends.

Was Brad suffocating Valiree mentally and emotionally?

"My dad gets mad at me for everything I do."

Well, it sounded to me as if Valiree was getting pretty upset, concerning her dad's behavior. I wondered why Valiree was taking 20 milligrams of Paxil. Was there some hiding going on?

An October 12, 1999, an entry in her diary described her frustration of how her father "won't leave me alone in my room" and "today he asked me if I wanted him to go out of my room."

Did Brad read Valiree's diary? Why was Valiree seeing a therapist?

Were she and Brad in therapy together? Did he know what Valiree was going to say during their session?

The next appointment was Monday, October 18th. Brad and Valiree were scheduled to see the therapist together, the day Valiree disappeared.

Coincidental? I think not. Evidence was stacking up.

Besides the pubic hairs found in Valiree's bedding, detectives found bedding, duct tape, a yellow tarp and three shovels inside a storage locker that Brad rented on South McDonald Road after his daughter's disappearance.

I heard about the contents of this affidavit on the evening news. I was spared a lot of footwork. Thank God for the news media.

❀ ❀ ❀

Brad's Girlfriend

"I talk to Brad every day."

That's what Brad's girlfriend told me on the phone Wednesday night. She said that she was still supporting Brad.

Hearing this really upset me. It was the way she talked about the whole situation. Here she was, still loving Brad, still "sticking to her man." Was she sympathizing with him, jeopardizing herself and her kids, calling it love? I just didn't get it.

Here was a woman, who was essentially Valiree's mom for two years, claiming that she was still in love with someone who is accused of murdering her. It didn't make any sense whatsoever. Wasn't she concerned about the safety of her own children?

Brad was telling her that he still loved her. He couldn't remember anything about what happened to Valiree and that she should know that he would never hurt his baby.

"Brad is scared of what might happen to him, but that he thinks he'll be found innocent."

How did he figure that?

Why would he even think that he would be found innocent with all the physical evidence against him?

133

I asked her if there could be some manipulating going there.

She was upset to see that Valiree's diary was made public. She didn't think that it should have been shown on TV.

"It's just circumstantial evidence—Valiree's journal can't convict Brad."

What mattered most to this woman was that he loved her as much as she loved him. Thirty minutes on the telephone with her was enough. I had heard enough.

❀ ❀ ❀

Understanding Legalities

Legal questions about Brad's trial were stirring my soul. So I tracked down an old high school basketball teammate who was a lawyer and picked his brain for answers.

"What were the chances of Brad's trial being moved from Spokane?"

"It's hard to say, but if it does happen it won't happen right away."

My friend explained that there would be some preliminaries and hearings that the judge would go through before the location could be changed.

"Could Brad get the lethal injection if he is convicted of murdering his daughter?"

"The only way that he would get capital punishment was if there was proven to be an aggravated count of the murder."

It wasn't enough that he violently murdered his daughter, but it has to be proven that he killed her to cover-up another crime. I thought maybe he did kill her to cover-up another crime. Why else would he kill her the way he did? I mean, her death was definitely not an accident. The medical examiner ruled that Valiree died of homicidal violence. He also told me that it appeared that she fought her attacker.

When Brad is convicted of first degree murder in the state of Washington, he will receive a maximum of 28 years of imprisonment. That ridiculous!

Dreams, Games, and Reports

I woke up Monday, December 6th, from another nightmare. I was finding my sister's remains, but I couldn't orient myself of where I had been nor what had happened to her. The pain in my face had returned.

However, dreams were one thing; reality was another. I knew that I would never rest until I knew what really happened to Roseann.

Was Brad responsible for my sister's death?

I contacted the jail that day to see if Brad would see me—not a chance.

That didn't surprise me, but I had to try.

The surprise came when officials announced that Brad remained on 24-hour suicide watch, which meant that officers checked on him at least every 15 minutes. What prompted this was finding out that Brad had torn his jail-issued blanket into strips. It looked as though he was planning to use the strips to make a noose and hang himself.

The prosecutor's office informed me that no semen was found on Valiree and that her hymen had not been broken. The report was in. However, just because the hymen was not broken, did not mean there was no molestation. It was still possible that sexual assault did take place. Proving it would be difficult, especially since there was no body.

❀ ❀ ❀

Where's Valiree's Mother?

I was looking for leads. I desperately wanted to solve my sister's disappearance. While I was concentrating on Brad's old house on Decatur, Gary Darigold the KHQ news reporter had uncovered another possible location where Brad was seen before with my sister. I heard the news on Tuesday, December 7th.

Residents at the house on 6th Avenue reported that their children had dug up a large bone several years ago in their yard. The address was that of Brad Jackson 's grandmother, Virginia. At the time of Roseann's disappearance, Brad also stayed at her house. He occupied the bedroom in the back corner of her home when he wasn't staying in his house on Decatur. The bone, I was told, looked like a human leg bone.

The owner's of the home were beside them-selves. They had lived right across the street in 1992 when Roseann disappeared. No one from the police station bothered to question them. No one bothered to tell them that Roseann had mysteriously disappeared. They knew Roseann and knew Valiree. They told me how sorry they were for my loses.

While watching the news they had seen that Brad had been arrested for the murder of Valiree. The news of Brad's arrest caused them to remember the leg bone that they found in their yard three to four years ago. They told me that if someone would have informed them seven years ago about Roseann's dis-appearance, they would not have thrown the bone away. They said, they would have gotten out there and dug, if the police didn't.

The news really rattled me. I was planning to leave on Friday, the day after Brad's arraignment. This discovery changed my plans.

The bone found brought back many emotions. It was like a dagger being shoved through my heart again.

A leg bone. God, have mercy. My Rose, my Rose's bone. Could it be?

My heart was aching again.

❀ ❀ ❀

The Cost of Valiree Jackson's Life

The Spokane prosecutors announced that they had found no evidence that justified seeking the death penalty against accused murderer William Brad Jackson.

It was rationalized that the death penalty option would be possible if the murder occurred concerning the rape of the child. Lab tests to establish whether Brad sexually assaulted his daughter were "not conclusive."

Of course, if "not conclusive" was only defined as an unbroken hymen, then rape still could have occurred. In my opinion, rape comes in many forms and should not be defined under one physical condition.

Spokane County detectives suggested that Brad sexually assaulted his daughter, then strangled her to prevent her from telling authorities about the abuse.

Shouldn't that qualify as an aggravating factor?

I knew that the prosecutors had to work within the boundaries of the law, regardless of their own personal feelings. I certainly appreciated their hard work.

A Weekend of Research

—Rape and sexual assault.

—Aggravated murder.

—Obstruction of justice.

I was spending my time during the weekend in the main library's law section trying to understand the legal ramifications of terms and definitions.

I was praying that I could help the prosecutors come up with something that would point towards aggravating circumstances that was needed for the State to seek the death penalty.

I couldn't understand why the prosecution wouldn't go after Aggravated Murder One. It didn't make sense to me to go a different way.

As it stands now, if Brad was to be convicted of Valiree's murder, prison would provide three square meals and snacks; TV, cable, and the Internet; exercise and medical attention; visiting privileges and phone calls; plenty of sleep and sunshine.

The Murder One charge without aggravating circumstances would offer the revolving door of crime for us to deal with. If convicted, Brad could go in, do his time, get rested up, come back out, and possibly commit another crime.

He would show up a little older and costlier to the taxpayer, and still be alive. I am appalled at that! I searched the law books for something— anything that would help the prosecution add aggravating circumstances to the charges against Brad.

❀ ❀ ❀

A Plus for the Prosecution

"The attorney for a Spokane Valley man accused of killing his 9-year-old daughter withdrew from the case."

Those were the words that I heard relayed to me from one of my news friends.

"Brad Jackson's lawyer is gone?"

The answer was affirmative.

The Spokane attorney withdrew from the case because Brad didn't have the money to hire private investigators and expert witnesses who were needed for his defense.

"Brad lost his job. He has no savings, no assets."

In fact, his parents even pulled their money from the case and decided not to spend their money on trying to defend their son. It sounded like they were finally wising up, or were they?

This meant that the trial date that was set for January 18th was postponed and the trial wouldn't begin until sometime in the fall of the year 2000.

What a relief. I thought that by that time maybe I could find Roseann and if he did kill her, then he could be tried for both mother and child. Brad was appointed a Public Defender, the taxpayers would pay for his defense.

The delay would give prosecutors and detectives longer to prepare their case against Brad. With time on their side, the prosecution had two words to say about how the situation, "It helped."
It helped a lot.

Winter Weather

We needed to get the digging done, I needed to find my sister.

Every day it was getting colder and colder and every day the ground could get harder and harder. I knew first-hand about Spokane winters. It could turn cold very quickly.

I called two different city detectives a couple times a day between December 8th and December 16th. I pleaded with them, "When are you going to dig? Every day the digging is put off, the ground gets harder and harder!"

One of the hip phrases in the 70's was "Can you dig it?" As a teenager, I remember sitting in the living room with Roseann while she braided my hair.

We would say back and forth, "Can you dig it, I can dig it too," jokingly while laughing together. I have many wonderful memories of my sister and Valiree that will be with me forever.

Since the dig site had been cleared and prepared all we could do was wait for the city detectives to do their job. In the meantime, I was preparing for a showdown with Brad— so to speak. I wanted to see him— you know, face to face. I know how our justice system works— slowly.

I believe that the Spokane prosecutors Steve Tucker and Jack Driscoll are preparing an overwhelming case against the accused. He will get his day in court and so will we. Until that time, there will be more preliminary hearings.

It was Tuesday, December 14th, at around 1:45 pm. I was at the courthouse for Brad's arraignment to upgrade his charges to Murder One.

❀ ❀ ❀

The Accused

I stepped into the courtroom at 1:50 while the judge was finishing up a case. I walked to the front and sat down quietly. Composure was essential for appearances.

The judge finished her case and as she left, all of us respectfully stood up. My sister Kathy came in around 1:55, saw me in the front, and walked up to sit beside me. I was glad she did.

As others were coming into the courtroom, I decided to walk out and catch a quick breath of fresh air. However, just as I turned around to leave— behold, four correction officers came in escorting, you-know-who.

My blood started boiling. I could feel my blood pressure rising. It had to be high. My face was twitching, my temples were throbbing; my heart was pounding.

I had the wrathful urge to grab Brad and shake him. I wanted to shake and shake and shake the truth out of him. I wanted all the lies that had been armored around him to fall away, leaving nothing but his bare soul. I wanted to do away with Darkness and Evil like never before. I wanted their destruction and I wanted it now. That's what Brad represented to me.

I sensed a presence or a force that held me back. I silently called upon Jesus for strength and inner peace. I was sinking and he pulled me up. I called on the name of Jesus and he was there, he was always there. There was only one set of "Footprints in the sand."

As Brad was escorted into the courtroom, I went back to the bench and sat down.

Brad's hands were handcuffed behind his back. He wore a gray, jail-issued jumpsuit.

It was a good thing that my sister sat between Brad and me, she was a good buffer to help me control the impulse I had to jump at him.

Brad was seated to the right of me in the front row. As he was sitting there, he looked over his left shoulder and caught my eye. I didn't bat an eyelash. I've wanted to look him in the eyes for years. He turned away too quickly for me to send a penetrating message to his heart. That's when I started taking deep breaths. My sister patted me on my shoulder.

"It's okay. It's okay."

I must have taken 15... 20... 30 deep breaths. They were very loud. What could I do? Everyone was looking and listening. The courtroom was quiet. All I could hear was my heavy breathing, and then the judge came in.

❀ ❀ ❀

Cool and Collected

The pressure was building so much— I stood up. As I moved to take my overcoat off, the police and the guards moved toward me. Maybe they thought that I was going to dive over my sister to get to Brad. It wasn't a bad idea, but I knew better.

I removed my overcoat and felt a little better. I wasn't as hot—that is, not as hot on the outside. Inside I was seething.

After the judge came in, she said a few words, then asked Brad how he pleaded.

"Not guilty."

No surprise there.

The hearing was over without incident.

The reporters came to me and asked how I felt and why I was there.

I had few words to say. For me to comment in the condition I was in was not a good idea. Thinking carefully and speaking slowly in a controlled voice, I said, "I wanted to see when Brad was going to trial because I wanted to be there. That's why I am here today."

I may have looked cool and collected, but I wasn't. I had to get out of the courthouse fast. I was seething and it was going to take hours to cool down.

Setting Up to Fail

Well, well, well. A Cadaver dog was finally going to make an appearance in the yard on East Sixth Avenue. This was Thursday, December 16th. If Roseann was to be found, I would have been very surprised. There were too many factors against having any success:

1) The detectives and dog were arriving after 4:00 pm. That meant less than 30 minutes of daylight.

2) It was a gloomy, cold day. The scent would be hard to pick up. The moisture in the ground would keep the scents from rising for a good detection.

Already I was making preparations to find Valiree's mother in the new year. I knew what had to be done. I wasn't giving up and I wasn't going away.

One of the city detectives said, "John we're not finished here yet. We will continue to look for Roseann."

For now, it was time to leave. I would be coming back for Roseann next year.

❀ ❀ ❀

"Mother and Child"

The days of the year were at their shortest. This meant Christmas was almost here. With Christmas being close to a week away, I wanted to get back to my wife and children. Besides, I was finding too many people in Spokane gone for the holidays. Things were shutting down and the holiday season was dictating time schedules. It was time to leave the city—at least for the time being.

As I got on the plane to fly back to Phoenix, I heard the joyous Christmas carols in the background. One traditional favorite kept repeating itself. Its music and words moved slowly through my mind, all the way home.

> Silent night, holy night
> All is calm, all is bright
> 'Round yon Virgin, Mother and Child
> Holy Infant, so tender and mild
> Sleep in heavenly peace
> Sleep in heavenly peace.

Indeed the night was becoming hushed as I looked out the window.

The bright lights of the city and of Christmas sparkled like stars below me. Above were the twinkling stars of the heavens. I found that darkness was casting its shadowy spell of silence over the city, silence that I had been feeling since I arrived in Spokane.

Things just weren't adding up yet. I wasn't feeling any calm about the closure of what had happened with my sister and my niece. I needed to find my sister's body and convict her killer. I needed to get the Valiree Jackson Bill written, passed, and enforced. If I was feeling any calm, it was more like, "the calm before the storm."

I will finish what I needed to finish as the days grow longer, the weather warms up, silence is broken, and the shadows fade away.

I knew that I would go back to Spokane in the new century. The year 2000 would be a fresh start in many ways.

❀ ❀ ❀

In memory of Valiree,
with the spirit of her mother,
We try to make better the world.
To walk through the darkness—
looking for hope,
To make the stars shine brighter above.
I hope to free, the lives of women
And lives of children to live—
Lives of love and lives of care with lives—
full of joy.
All will be calm and all will be right,
when this comes to be.
Then Roseann and Valiree will be able to
sleep— then, in heavenly peace.
They will sleep in peace as mother and child,
This will not be just be words,
That we hear once a year,
They will be for real— now and forever.
Mother and child, Roseann and Valiree,
Will sleep— in heavenly peace.

❀ ❀ ❀

❀ ❀ ❀

What Can We Do?

I truly do not understand and I say this from my heart, why a child would be considered less of a victim than a police officer. I just don't understand that if an officer is killed in the line of duty, it automatically becomes a case for the death penalty. I believe the same punishment should go for anyone who murders a child.

Many children are being abused and sexually assaulted every day. Moreover, it is not just in Spokane, it is national and worldwide.

As individuals in our homes and leaders in our communities, we must initiate action. We must not tolerate murderers, especially those who murder children. We must unite to make the change to cast that evil out of this world.

As we enter the new millennium, Valiree Jackson's message is loud and clear. We need to look after our children. We need to pay closer attention to signs that hint at child abuse and neglect. We must keep watch of the children. There are those among us that have completely crossed over to Darkness. They could be your neighbor, a friend, or even a family member. If you notice any suspicious behavior or actions or words, then please, tell someone.

that have completely crossed over to Darkness. They could be your neighbor, a friend, or even a family member. If you notice any suspicious behavior or actions or words, then please, tell someone. Report it! Follow up on it.

Organizations will help. All you have to do is ask and if that doesn't work, then ask again and again and again. We must not give up.

What will become of the children whose danger we ignore or deny? What will happen if we mind our own business, if we don't want to get involved? If nothing changes and improves, if inaction is acceptable and remains the status quo, then more children will also be victimized as Valiree was. More and more children will suffer as we wipe our hands from it all and shake our heads in disbelief and disgust. Nothing gets done with wiping and shaking.

In other words, the more wiping and shaking and excuses, the more children will die, like Valiree. More child killers will get away with murder.

We must stand and mean "NO MORE!"

We must show that Valiree's message has strength in its punishment: The killing of children demands imprisonment without parole or it demands the death penalty.

Please help me, help the children by passing a bill into law that would make murdering a child a capital offense. If you're against the death penalty then how about "life in prison without parole?"

Senator Jim West, one of Washington State's finest, will be helping me with the "Valiree Jackson Bill." Mark Fuhrman and Mike Fitzsimmons from KXLY Radio

920 were the first individuals to help me initiate the Bill. They were very encouraging.

My family and friends will continue to help me search for my sister. Your prayers are needed and appreciated. If she was a victim of a serial killer, as first thought by the Spokane Police, then we should know something soon.

Spokane like many other cities is a beautiful place with wonderful people. Together we can rid our communities of such crimes against humanity. This must be our common goal, one for all and all for one.

While we're saving our children— we're saving our future.

❀ ❀ ❀

A TRIBUTE TO VALIREE

After Valiree's disappearance and subsequent death, the children at her school McDonald Elementary, put their feelings into words and drawings.

The following poems and drawings were presented to me by one of Valiree's teachers after her funeral. I trust that they will bring as much comfort to you as they've brought to me.

For the short period that Valiree spent with the children at McDonald Elementary, their love for her echoes through their own words and pictures.

SAFELY HOME

I am now at home in heaven;
      All's so happy, all so bright!
There is perfect joy and beauty
      In this everlasting light.
All the pain and grief are over,
      Every restless tossing past;
I am now at peace forever,
      Safely home in heaven at last
Did you wonder I so calmly
      Trod the Valley of the Shade?
Oh! But Jesus' love illumined
      Every dark and fearful glade.
And He came Himself to meet me
      In that way so hard to tread;
And with Jesus' arm to lean on,
      Could I have one doubt or dread?
Then you must not grieve so sorely,
      For I love you dearly still;
Try to look beyond earth's shadows,
      Pray to trust our Father's will.
There is work still waiting for you
      So you must not idle stand;
Do your work while life remaineth--
      You shall rest in Jesus' land
When that work is all completed,
      He will gently call you home;
Oh, the rapture of the meeting!
      Oh, the joy to see you come!

The Valiree We Loved

She came here in March to McDonald School
The kids in her class all thought she was cool

Her curly red hair sure made her stand out
Very soon she fit in without any doubt

Even though a new school is hard at the start
Valiree made friends, she gave from the heart

Her brown eyes they twinkled whenever she smiled
She was thoughtful and caring to every child

Besides being kind, she was also so bright
Her work was well done, a teacher's delight

Such a warm little girt, we wish we could save
Her smile, her charm, and the hugs that she gave

As time goes along, she'll live on in our hearts
We'll smile and remember, she was a big part

Of the class who will miss her when day after day
Her desk sits there empty, her things put away

We'll miss her, our Valiree, our lives she has
touched
Goodbye, little Valiree, we loved you so much.

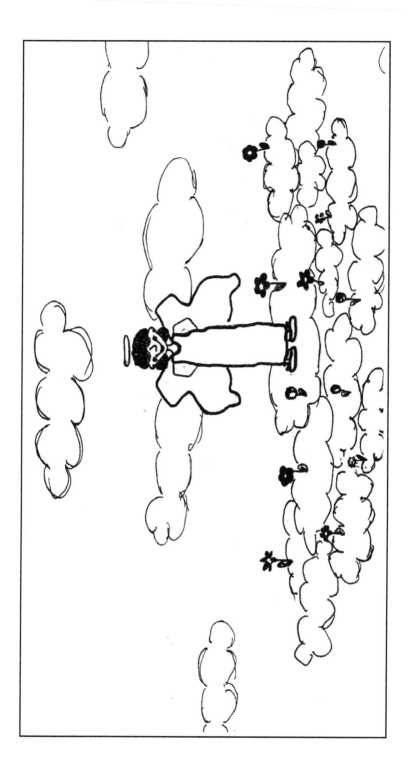

Shes in a Magical Place!

Valiree is in all of our hearts!!! We will never forget what happend to nine year old Valiree. She takes space in all of us. She will become a part of the kingdome of Heaven, and will never be forgoten! ♦

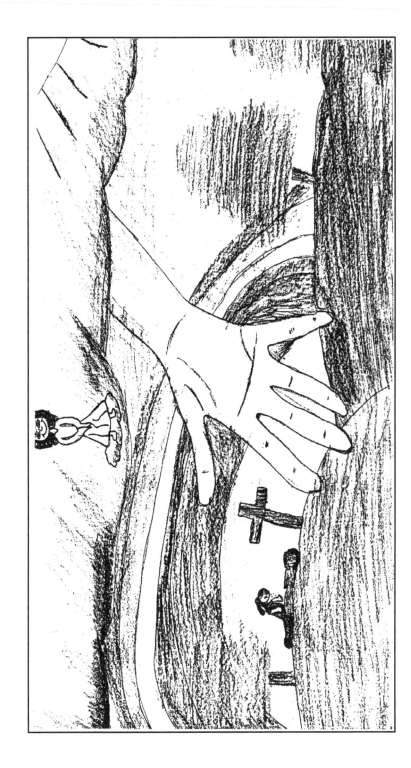

She's not gone forever

She's not gone forever
I know she's in a better
place
When the wind blows
I will remember you
When the stars glow I
will think about you
I will never forget
you Valincia
No matter what people
say you do.

to: Valincia Jackson

with lots of love of care

Hands of the Heavens Reach Down

There are hands
Hands of the heavens
They take beautiful lives
Lives of people in pain

Reaching down to the world
Taking the hurt out the people
And bring them to a magical place
Where they live forever

There are hands
Hands of the heavens
They take beautiful lives
Lives of people in pain

Her first look at life lasted 9 years
She is now looking down on us
And keeping us safe
I will never forget her

There are hands
Hands of the heavens
They take beautiful lives
Lives of people in pain

Even though your body has died
Your spirit lives on
You are not in pain anymore
We miss you Valiree.

A rose in the bottom of the ocean

You are like a rose at the bottom of the sandy ocean.
When I think of you my heart beats
of heartache and pain.
Now you are gone and now youre in a wonderfuly
place.
Even though I did not know you you'll always be my
friend.
When the birds sing over the ocean they're telling
you and wishing you a happy and wonderful feeling
That youre not alone.
You'll always be in my heart and my Sissters heart
too.
God will be there for when your hurt or when a
petal comes off.
When I think of you my heart hurts and aches a
a lot.
When I know that your not gone and that you'll always
be in my heart.
You'll always have an angel with you wherever you go.
You are in heaven were angels are with you.

VALTREE JACKSON

There are holes in the floor of heaven. And her tears are pouring down rain. That's how we all know she is watching. Wishing that she could be with us now.

She's in a magical place now. Heaven is where that is. She touched a lot of people's lives. They miss her so much.

She's an angel up in heaven. And she just earned her wings. They are spread out wide. Remember her soft brown eyes that gleamed.

We all miss you Valtree. Your soul lives in our memories. It will live on and on Goodbye, but not for too long.

Like The Wind

You are like the wind,
You came and went,
We will miss you alot,
But your not gone forever.

You went to a better place,
Where there is no violence,
Your gardian angle's there,
Your not gone forever.

You are a part of our lives,
You will always be with us,
Although your body is dead,
Your spirit lives forever.

All the things you have done,
Everything you have seen,
You lived life to the fullest eacl
I will appreciate life twice as mu

You are like the wind,
You came and went,
We will miss you alot,
But your not gone forever.

A New Life Has Just Begun

Valiree Jackson is a name I'll never
forget
She is a star in the sky that is watching
over us
Even though she is gone
She will always be in my heart.

When the clouds open up to the
heavens
She has been lifted up into the
sky
And now as she recieves her wings
She can visit us again.

She has been born into the kingdom
of heaven.
I wonder if she is playing in the snow
Or even jumping in the leaves
Now the pain is gone and a very lucky
child has Valiree as a guardian angel.

So farwell my dear, dear, Valiree
Please protect us while your in the
sky
We will miss you
And I know your not gone forever.

She's Not Gone Forever

She's not gone forever
Only to a better place
No words can describe
That beautiful kingdom
Up high in the clouds
She's much happier there
Where theres no violence,
    or sickness
No hurt, or pain
Everything is perfect

I can hear her laughing
    now
Playing with all the angels
    in heaven
Jumping from cloud to cloud
Sun shining brilliantly all
    around her
Engulfing her in it's warmth
Clear, blue sky overhead
Nothing could be better
I'm so happy she's in such
A wonderful place!

Life is a Gift

Life is a gift,
Celebrate life,
 Enjoy each day to the fullest,
Before it's too late.

Achieve high goals,
Always try your best,
Learn all you can,
Before it's too late.

Meet new friends,
Have lots of friends,
Be nice to them,
Before it's too late.

Don't start fights,
Don't get involved with gangs,
Don't fight make peace,
Before it's too late.